P9-CQA-851

Mary's Unveiled Heart

a true story

Mary's Unveiled Heart

Mary Bucy

Pleasant Word
A Division of WinePress Group
PW

© 2009 by Mary Bucy. All rights reserved.

Pleasant Word (a division of WinePress Publishing, PO Box 428, Enumclaw, WA 98022) functions only as book publisher. As such, the ultimate design, content, editorial accuracy, and views expressed or implied in this work are those of the author.

No part of this publication may be reproduced, stored in a retrieval system, or transmitted in any way by any means—electronic, mechanical, photocopy, recording, or otherwise—without the prior permission of the copyright holder, except as provided by USA copyright law.

Unless otherwise noted, all Scriptures are taken from the *Holy Bible, New International Version®, NIV®*. Copyright © 1973, 1978, 1984 by the International Bible Society. Used by permission of Zondervan. All rights reserved.

Scripture references marked KJV are taken from the King James Version of the Bible.

Scripture references marked NASB are taken from the New American Standard Bible, © 1960, 1963, 1968, 1971, 1972, 1973, 1975, 1977 by The Lockman Foundation. Used by permission.

ISBN 13: 978-1-4141-1261-9
ISBN 10: 1-4141-1261-0
Library of Congress Catalog Card Number: 2008906019

*This book is dedicated
to the heroes of my heart*

*my mortal hero
my husband
Steve Bucy*

and

*my Immortal Hero
my Savior
Jesus Christ*

Contents

A multitude of people have added their brush strokes to the mural that is my life. I wish I could thank each one, but it would take a thousand pages.

Without doubt, Jesus has been the Artist. He has creatively painted my life in ways I could never have imagined. All my praise and thanks goes to this One who saved my soul, who literally saved my life.

My dreams never would have come true if God had not gifted me with the incredible man I call my husband. Steve, you are the love of my life. You have impacted me in ways that are beyond imagination. Your love has been the constant in my life when everything around me was falling apart. Thank you for cherishing me, forgiving me, introducing me to Jesus, demonstrating grace, making life fun and exciting, believing in me, and helping me to grow as a woman after God's own heart. I am who I am today because of you.

The jewels in my crown are my four children: Sarah Therese Klingler, Ruthanne Elisabeth Kirk, Hester Catherine Dailey, and Micah Benjamin Bucy. You each are precious gifts from my Heavenly Father. Thank you for being patient with me while God was teaching me how to be a mother. Thank you for persevering, enduring, and growing in grace along with your dad and me on one of the greatest adventures of our lives as missionaries in the Philippines. I am so very proud of each one of you! Most of all, I thank you for giving me the most awesome gift a mother could ask for—knowing that my children walk with the Lord.

I must thank my three sons-in-law: Brandon Klingler, Ryan Kirk, and Dale Dailey for loving my daughters. You each have added so much to our family with your individual and unique personalities, talents, and gifts. Thanks for your willingness to marry into our family, knowing what a strange mother-in-law you would have!

My four grandchildren: Audrey Paige Kirk, Elena Grace Klingler, Madelyn Rose Kirk, and Paul Steven Klingler. Thank you for being my joy in this season of my life. "I love you, Grandma," must be the sweetest words in the world!

My mother: Anna Klopp McDermott Zusky. You carried me in your womb for nine months, brought me into the world in pain, and nurtured me through my childhood. Thank you for the sacrifices you made. You loved me even when I took your only grandchildren 10,000 miles away to the Philippines. The Bible says in the book of Joel, chapter two, "I will repay you for the years the locusts have eaten…and you will praise the name of the Lord your God, who has worked wonders for you." God is repaying you now by surrounding you with family who loves you, including your four great-grandchildren. Thanks, to both you and Dorla Lukens, for your persistence and encouragement in publishing my letters.

[Jesus called my mother Home on September 6, 2008.]

My best friend: Joan Davies. God knew all along—He kept throwing us together until we finally listened to Him. We've been through so much. You know all my secrets (and I know all yours!). Your care for Sarah and Ruthanne when we sent them home from the Philippines to attend college has definitely earned you rewards that are awaiting you in heaven. Thank you with all my heart! Your friendship means more to me than you'll ever know—you are the sister I never had.

My cousin: Sally Scala. You have been an important part of my life since childhood, because you've been more than a cousin—you have been a friend. So many of my memories include you—happy ones (you as my Matron of Honor at my wedding, the births of our children) and painful ones (the deaths of our parents). Your thoughtfulness, love, and compassion have touched my heart. Thank you for always being there for me.

My prayer circle: Sharon Aten, Lori Johnson, Linda Thompson, Marcia Miller, Margo Haren, Karen Hamilton, and Mary Homsher. You were my lifeline during our last four years in the Philippines. Although you individually prayed for us during our previous three terms, together you were a force to be reckoned with in our fourth term. Thank you for praying me back to the mission field, praying me through my best years as a missionary, praying me back home again, and then continuing to pray me through the challenges of readjusting to American life, which included God's gift of a home in Hartville ("Heart"-ville)! I am indebted to you.

My spiritual mentor: Sally Mittelstadt. You were very much my "savior" during my first term in the Philippines. You encouraged, you prayed, you counseled, you weren't shocked by the things I told you. As I grew over the years, you became more than a mentor—you became a friend. Thank you for investing time in me and for believing in me.

My missionary friend: Felicia Friesen. Your friendship has meant so much to me, especially in our last four years in the Philippines. You were my kindred spirit as we laughed, cried, rejoiced, encouraged, prayed, had fun together, and challenged each other! Thank you. You remain a treasured friend.

My Filipina friends: Ana Salvosa, Mimi Cristobal, Menchie DeSeo, Dorcas Fernandez, and Lani Valdez. I have a picture sitting on my desk of the six of us at Sonya's Garden in Tagaytay. It makes me smile and reminds me of my sisters in Christ who loved and accepted this crazy American. Thank you for showing me that culture does not matter when the hearts of women are connected. *Maraming salamat po!*

My prayer partners: Ayesha Nurruddin, Lois Pivato, and Dorla Lukens. My recent journey into the past was a difficult one. You prayed me through the fears and tears, and then you rejoiced with me when I came out on the other side in freedom. Thank you for walking with me, and for allowing me to walk with you, as we travel through life together.

My pastors: Dave Burnham, Knute Larson, and Paul Sartarelli. You have blessed my life immensely. Thank you for your faithfulness in teaching truth, infusing grace, and modeling the love of Christ for me and my family.

My three heroines: Sue Burnham, Jeanine Larson, and Pat Pacheco. You each have been such godly examples to me as women, as mothers, as daughters, but most importantly, as pastors' wives. Thank you for being such wonderful role models. I want to be like you when I grow up!

My special friend and "elbow": Susie Sartarelli. You encouraged, challenged, inspired, motivated, and prompted me to remove the veil from my heart and tell my story, all the while praying for me to have the courage to do so. You have been a critical part of my journey to peace and freedom. Thank you with all my heart!

My friend: Gail Benn. You are a woman of integrity. I trusted you with the concerns of my heart, and you listened without judging. Thank you for faithfully praying for me. I so appreciate you and your tender, compassionate heart.

It is my joy and privilege to introduce to you Mrs. Mary Bucy. She has been connected to my life for over 40 years—36 as my beloved wife! We remain today God's good work through Jesus, progressing in our marriage journey toward Christ-likeness. As we walk together, we continue to extend both forgiveness and love, out of the humility that has come from the personal brokenness of the soul because of sin.

Our desire today is knowing Christ Jesus our Lord, walking in His love, and experiencing the delight of living together as joint heirs of the grace of life.

I commend Mary to you as a fellow pilgrim, struggling servant, and growing sojourner—one who is learning to live out her faith in the frailty of the human heart and the difficulty of human relationships, but doing so with refreshing truth, a brutal honesty, and with the strength, vulnerability, and perseverance of her Savior.

My prayer is that God will use her life's story—the forthrightness of our struggles and the overcoming we have experienced through Jesus—and that the Spirit of the living God will impart to your hearts both the courage to face life's greatest challenges and the commitment to be fully devoted followers of the Good Shepherd. Please listen now to Mary's heart, and may you, too, be the trophy of His grace.

To God be the glory!

Steve Bucy
2008

My Purpose
my heart's desire

When I originally began opening my heart and sharing my journal writings with other missionary women several years ago, it was with a Colossians 2:2–7 purpose in mind: that they might be "encouraged in heart, knit together in love, rooted and built up in Christ, strengthened in the faith, and overflowing with thankfulness."

I was later encouraged and motivated to write my story through the promptings of a friend and then from what I believe was God's Spirit speaking to me at a Beth Moore conference. The topic for the conference was "Get out of that pit." One of the texts Beth used spoke directly to my heart. It was 2 Corinthians 3:7–18. She focused on the last four verses: "Even to this day when Moses is read, a veil covers their hearts. But whenever anyone turns to the Lord, the veil is taken away. Now the Lord is the Spirit, and where the Spirit of the Lord is there is freedom. And we, who with unveiled faces all reflect the Lord's glory, are being transformed into His likeness with ever increasing glory, which comes from the Lord, who is the Spirit." Beth was adamant about the responsibility we have, once we are out of our pits, to unveil our hearts, make ourselves vulnerable, and share with others how Christ has rescued us. In the days following the conference, I read those verses over and over, continuing on through 2 Corinthians 4. The words went straight to my heart. After much prayer and counsel from my husband, I took a leap of faith by writing my story.

It is now my heart's desire and my prayer that as you join me on my journey of faith and my path to freedom, as you read my story, analyze my letters, and examine my favorite

Scripture verses, as you become aware of God's unending love, amazing grace, and divine mercy at work in my life—*you would see Jesus*!

My Story
my heart's journey of faith

The cemetery was quiet except for the traffic passing by just outside the gate. I was hardly aware of any noise, though, because there were too many thoughts rattling around in my head. The sun shone brightly in an ocean of puffy white clouds, reminding me of the beautiful summer days of my childhood. The grass was prickly under my legs. I pulled up small clumps and tossed them away from me in frustration. I desperately needed to talk to my daddy, but we had buried him 40 years ago in the grave I was sitting next to.

I never got to know him as an adult. I was a teenager when he died. He was a quiet man, my dad. Though he never talked about the war, his experiences in World War II had an emotional impact on him. He was not very affectionate, but I'm pretty sure he loved me. My mom said I was the apple of his eye. I was their only child. I have a picture of me sitting on his lap when I was a little girl. So, yes, I'm pretty sure he loved me. I just wish he would have told me.

I only saw my dad cry three times. The first was when his mother died. Grandma lived with us in our small, two-bedroom apartment. She and I shared a bedroom. I fell safely asleep each night with her lying in the twin bed next to mine. I loved her so much. A lifetime of fears began the day she died. It happened on a cold January afternoon shortly after I got home from school. My mom had gone to pick my dad up at work. Grandma was sitting on a stool talking to her niece on the telephone. Two of my cousins were at our place, and we were sitting at a small table in the living room eating a snack. The television was on. We were laughing about some silly antics when I heard a loud crash. I turned around and saw Grandma crumpled on the floor. I jumped out of my chair to help her. She was conscious, but unable to get up. She told me to call her niece back. Everything happened so quickly after that. Several relatives arrived, taking charge, relieving me of the overwhelming responsibility of caring for my grandmother. An ambulance soon pulled up in front of our apartment. As they wheeled her out on a stretcher, I took one last look at Grandma. Her face was so pale. Her eyes were closed. It frightened me to see her like that. My dad and mom arrived home shortly after the ambulance left. They sped off to the hospital, and I was sent to my cousins' apartment just a block away. I ended up spending the night. The next morning I strolled home expecting to get ready for school, not aware that my grandmother had died during the night. The sadness that greeted me as I walked in the door was so heavy that you could almost reach out and grab it. When I saw the tears on my dad's cheeks, I knew that something terrible had happened. I started crying, my little heart broken, when I was told of Grandma's death.

A few days later, at the funeral home, a well-meaning aunt made me go up to the casket and kiss my grandmother goodbye. Her cheek was so cold. This was not my warm, sweet, cuddly grandma. A terror that I had never experienced before shot through my heart. My nine-year-old mind could not fully wrap itself around the concept of death. The only thing I really understood was that my grandmother would never again hug me to her ample bosom. I would never again fall asleep with her lying in the bed across the room.

I honestly do not remember much of what happened after the funeral, except that I was afraid that my mommy or daddy might die, too. I had trouble sleeping. I missed my grandmother so much. There was no gentle snoring in the other bed to lull me to sleep at night.

Life continued on as it tends to do even when it seems the world should stop because someone is missing. The days turned into months and the months into years. Grandma faded into the past as I entered my teen years. When I was a sophomore at Garfield High School, in September, 1966, a blue-eyed, blond-haired boy came into my life. Steve was so incredibly cute that every time he looked at me with those baby blue eyes I thought for sure my heart would beat right out of my chest. When he asked me to dance at a Hi-Teens dance at the YMCA one Thursday evening, I couldn't believe it! And then when he walked me home afterwards and kissed me goodnight, I knew I was in love. My heart was his! Though our relationship had its ups and downs, as most teenage relationships do, except for the summer of 1967, we dated all through high school.

My life was fun and busy during those high school days with my boyfriend, friends, dances, football games at the Rubber Bowl, cruising down the Boulevard, LuJann's Drive-in, parties, basketball games, and all the other normal teenage activities of the 1960s. I suppose I wasn't much interested in spending time at home with my parents. For one thing, it wasn't easy to have a conversation with my father, who seemed to find it increasingly difficult to relate to me as a teenager. But there was still the security in knowing that he and my mother would be there when I came home. Until, on that fateful day in March, 1968, that security was pulled out from under my feet when my dad was diagnosed with cancer, and he was given three to six months to live.

The next months were extremely stressful. My mom cared for Dad at home as long as she could. She had to feed him through a tube in his stomach. Many nights I woke up to his screams of agony. The area around the tube was so painful he said it felt like it was on fire. He grew so frail and weak. Often during the day and night he had trouble breathing, and we would have to sit him up so he could catch his breath. He and my mom both slept downstairs in the living room on two different parts of a sectional couch. Mom was so exhausted from caring for Dad during the day that she fell into a deep sleep at night. Dad had a hard time waking her up when he couldn't breathe, so Mom finally tied a rope with bells on it between her couch and his. I would jump out of bed in a panic when awakened at night by the jingling of those bells.

When Mom needed to run out to the grocery store, I would stay with Dad. I was so scared that he would die while I was home alone with him. I couldn't help remembering that in this same living room, eight years earlier, I had sat with my grandmother after she suffered a stroke. On one of those days that I was sitting with Dad, I saw him cry for the second time. Through tears he asked me, "I'm going to die, aren't I?" I felt like someone punched me in the stomach. My mom had chosen not to tell him he had cancer and only a few months to live. So what was I supposed to say? I just couldn't tell him the truth, so I said, "No, Dad, you're going to get better." Maybe there was still the glimmer of hope in my heart that he would get better. I had been praying and pleading with God to please let him live. Surely He would hear my prayers.

On June 8, three months after the cancer diagnosis, I woke up to find my aunt and uncle downstairs. During the night, I somehow slept through the commotion of an ambulance, without the siren, coming to the apartment and taking Dad to the hospital. I didn't eat breakfast that morning. I rushed out of the apartment, but by the time I reached the hospital, Dad was already in a coma. Mom and I sat vigil with him for the rest of that day. Sitting there, gazing out the window, I thought about how much I had wanted to hear my dad tell me he loved me before he died. Maybe he had told me some time in the past. I couldn't remember. But I also could not remember if I, in all my seventeen years, had ever told him that I loved him. As I sat next to the hospital bed, I took his hand in mine and whispered in his ear, "I love you, Dad." A tear fell down his cheek. This was the third and last time I ever saw him cry. Even though he was in a coma, I'm convinced he heard my words. Was that tear his way of saying he loved me? Maybe. I don't know. But I have held onto that memory for 40 years. Not long after, I saw his chest rise and fall as he took his last breath. My daddy was gone at the young age of 47. And at that moment there was such an anger burning in my heart toward God that I felt physically sick to my stomach.

My boyfriend Steve was my savior during this terrible time of grief. He was always there for me. Unfortunately, my mother was not. She was having enough trouble dealing with her own grief and did not see how Dad's death was affecting me. I understood, and I harbored no bitterness toward her. However, her absence in my life resulted in much pain and fear. She went to work in the morning, and because she hated coming home to our apartment in the evening, she usually went out with her sister, not returning home until sometimes two or three o'clock in the morning. I spent many nights alone in that lonely apartment. There were nights when I lay awake in the darkness, afraid that she would not come home at all. I had nightmares every night about my dad and death and evil. Spiritually I was far from the Lord. I stopped going to church because I felt that God had turned His back on me. How could I possibly trust someone who had taken my father away? If it wasn't for Steve, I'm not sure I would have survived those days.

Once again life marched on. Steve and I were very much in love, and in September, 1972, we were married in our local Catholic church. I had attended the parochial grade school connected to that church for eight years, and even though I wasn't interested in the things of God, having the wedding in the church was just the thing to do. It was a day of mixed emotions—happiness that I was marrying my high school sweetheart, but sadness that my dad was not there to walk me down the aisle. After we said our vows, I remember thinking that I would never be alone again. Steve would always be there when I went to sleep at night.

We settled in, learning to adjust to married life. Steve had a well-paying job at Firestone Tire and Rubber Company and continued to attend the University of Akron. I worked for an ophthalmologist. When our first child was born in November, 1973, we were so excited. Though I suffered a bit from "baby blues," life in general was good. Good, that is, until the day Steve came home from work and told me that he had been put on night shift. "No, no," I screamed. "This can't be happening." I had finally felt secure falling asleep at night next to my husband, and that security was abruptly taken away from me. The nightmares returned with a vengeance, and all the old fears came crashing in on me again as I was forced to spend nights alone. Sleepless nights, and sleepless days caring for a new baby, took their toll on me. I was physically and emotionally exhausted. As the days turned into months, my fears grew.

It was right around this time that the movie *The Exorcist* came out. I knew better than to go see it, but many of my friends had, and they didn't hesitate to talk about it. Of course, they knew nothing of what I was going through. I began to wonder if maybe I was demon possessed like the girl in the movie.

Steve, bless his heart, didn't know how to deal with my fears. I pleaded with him to get off night shift, but it was out of his control. He was trying his best to be a good husband, father, and provider. In fact, there were days that he would work overtime and sometimes double overtime in order to provide for us and to save enough money to buy a house. Though I still loved him, I found myself growing angrier and angrier with him as my fears intensified. He did not seem to understand the torment I was going through and how deep the fears were embedded in my heart. I was not thinking rationally, and I am sad to say, I turned to another man. This adulterous affair was short-lived. I'm not sure what I expected. If I thought this would alleviate the fears and loneliness, I was wrong. On the contrary, it made matters worse. The guilt was more than I could handle. The shame I experienced compounded the turmoil that was already present in my heart and soul.

My fears escalated to terror. I was almost paralyzed with fright during the nights to the point that I could hardly function. Then one night I was so scared that I ran from the apartment with my baby in my arms. I spent the rest of the night lying on the floor of a friend's apartment. The next morning, when Steve came home from work, he found the note I had hurriedly scribbled and came to pick us up. Although he did not know about my transgression, he realized that my problem was bigger than either one of us could cope with. It was time to seek help. We made an appointment with the parish priest. I went with great anticipation that I would finally find relief. Much to my disappointment, when I asked the priest about demon possession, he just laughed. He did not take me seriously and was not able to give me any answers, let alone any hope. This strengthened my earlier resolve to have nothing to do with the church.

A friend who knew I was going through some struggles suggested Transcendental Meditation. I decided to give it a try. I can still remember walking into the house in West Akron where I would learn to "meditate." A young man took me upstairs to a room where an altar was set up. A white cloth and a picture of a maharajah adorned this altar. My "teacher" asked me for the items I was instructed to bring: flowers, a piece of fruit, and a clean white handkerchief. He proceeded to perform some sort of ritual, telling me it was not necessary for me to participate. I chose not to, trying to convince myself I was not there for religious purposes. I only wanted to learn how to relax and take my mind off my fears. When he had finished his "offering" he gave me my mantra, emphasizing that I was not to reveal it to anyone. He showed me how to meditate—how to sit with my eyes closed repeating my mantra over and over again. This caused a weird floating, out-of-the-body sensation to come over me. A warning bell went off in my head, but I ignored it.

During the next several weeks, I made the effort to meditate every day. My attempt, though, to dispel my fears was not successful. TM was not working for me, so I gave it up. Years later I learned that my mantra was actually the name of a Hindu god. I shudder every time I think of calling on a false god, leaving myself open to Satan's influence.

The day finally came when I could no longer carry the burden of my secret. I confessed my sin to my husband. I will never ever forget the look of pain and betrayal on Steve's face. Nor will I forget his words that pierced my heart. "But Mary, you were my rock."

My fears continued, but now there was another fear heaped on top of those—the fear that Steve would never be able to forgive me. I was terrified that he would leave me. But he stayed, and he did forgive me. His forgiveness and commitment and love gave me hope that we could start anew. It was an extremely difficult time, battling my insecurities and trying to earn his trust and respect again. During this rebuilding of our relationship, we were both striving to be good spouses and good parents, but we were finding it overwhelming in our own strength. Something was missing, and we had no idea what it was. Part of the problem was my fears that just would not go away. The friend who had suggested TM recommended a priest at St. Thomas Hospital who dealt with alcoholics. Although there was no alcohol involved in our situation, we figured it was worth a try. At the first appointment he asked me to get a complete physical examination to make sure I was healthy. I complied, and the results were good. During our second visit with the priest, he made the statement that he believed my problem was spiritual. He handed me a Gospel of John. Never before had a priest suggested I read the Bible.

Steve and I took this seriously, and we both attempted to read the Bible. Unfortunately, we really did not understand what we were reading. Since the priest had implied that my fears stemmed from spiritual issues, I thought it best that I return to the Catholic Church. I went to confession, where, after saying my penance, I was "absolved" of my sin. I attended Mass every week. Even though Steve did not go to church with me, he had been trying to "turn over a new leaf," especially because he was going to be a father again. I was pregnant with our second child.

On April 30, 1976, Steve found out the hard way that he was not capable of turning over a new leaf. He attended the bachelor party of a high school friend. It was a night of drinking and marijuana and fighting. When he came home in the early hours of May 1, he had reached bottom. His own depravity had hit him between the eyes.

Firestone was on strike at the time, and Steve was scheduled to picket later that morning. When I drove him to the gate where he was to picket, though he didn't know it, he was ready for his "divine appointment." Because it was raining, he sat in the car of his co-worker. And for six hours he heard the good news of Jesus Christ. Before he got out of the car, he prayed the salvation prayer, confessing his sins and asking Jesus to be his Savior and Lord. When I picked him up after attending Saturday Mass, a new man got into my car. I had thought he might be in a bad mood caused by a hangover and having to picket in the rain. But what I saw took my breath away. Steve's face was radiant! The very first thing he did was tell me what had happened to him.

Even though this seemed like it should have been a good thing, it initially fueled the fires of my insecurity and fear of losing my husband. When he went to church at The Chapel the next morning and didn't come home for hours, I thought he had been kidnapped by a cult, and I just knew I would never see him again. But he did come home. Over the next weeks, I observed the changes in Steve. He had a peace that I never saw in him before, a peace that I desperately wanted. Finally, my curiosity got the better of me, and I decided to see exactly what this was all about. The Chapel was like nothing I had ever experienced before. There was something in that building that was drawing me. But I was not yet ready to leave the Catholic Church. So I attended Mass on Saturday afternoons and The Chapel on Sunday mornings until the truth of God's Word penetrated my heart and my soul. Steve had never pressured me, and the only thing I can say is that he prayed and loved me into the Kingdom of Light. On July 4 of the same year, I gave my heart and my life to Jesus Christ after I realized that there was absolutely nothing I could do to earn eternal life. This was contrary to the teaching I received growing up. Good works would not help get me to heaven. It was only through faith in Jesus Christ who willingly died on the cross to pay for my sins. I may have gone to confession months earlier, confessing my sins to a priest, but true repentance came as a response to the Spirit of God and not to a set of rules.

I wish I could say that my life was suddenly and radically changed. Though my husband's transformation seemed to be immediate, mine has been much more gradual. I had to readjust my concept of God and His character. I had to learn to trust the One who I thought had betrayed me when my dad died. This continues to be an ongoing process for me. My fears and insecurities did not vanish instantly. It has been a long, hard battle.

Two years after our conversion, my husband sensed that the Lord was redirecting our lives and that he was being called into full-time ministry. The following year we moved to Chicago so Steve could attend Moody Bible Institute. We had two children, and I was pregnant with our third. Halfway through our three years in Chicago, Steve once again sensed the Lord redirecting our lives—this time to overseas missions. After graduation we moved to Columbia, South Carolina, so Steve could get further training. A year-and-a-half later, we were back in the Akron area to continue our preparation for moving to another country. Our fourth child was born while Steve was doing an internship at The Chapel. Then the day came in 1986 when we boarded the airplane with our four children and flew to the Philippines to begin our missionary career.

It would be a wonderful thing if I could claim that I willingly went to the Philippines out of love and complete obedience to the Lord. But I would be lying. Though my heart very much wanted to be obedient to the Lord, my motivation was not that honorable. I went out of fear. I went because this was what Steve wanted to do. I didn't really want to go to the Philippines, but I did want to please my husband. I was still afraid of losing him. It was evident that I had never fully dealt with the old insecurities, the doubts and apprehensions, the guilt and the shame. In retrospect, I realize that I had never truly forgiven myself for the sin against my husband. Though Steve said he had forgiven me, and I knew that God had forgiven me, I was still trying to pay for my sin.

Our first term in this foreign country was a living nightmare. Not only did I not want to be there, but also I lost my identity. I didn't know who I was. My fears resurfaced, especially those in the spiritual realm. This shouldn't have been surprising since the culture was steeped in animism and fear of evil spirits, even within the context of Catholicism.

Many difficult things transpired during our first year in the Philippines. Our 20-month-old son was attacked by a monkey that bit him seven times on the head. We lived in a town that was permeated with a spiritual oppression. Severe asthma attacks resulted in our son being hospitalized twice. Our two oldest daughters (7th grade and 5th grade) were in a missionary kids' boarding school two hours away from where we lived. Home schooling our youngest daughter for the first time caused much anxiety. I worried that she would be far behind her classmates when she started second grade at Faith Academy the following year. Sickness. Culture shock. Pressure to learn the language. Live-in house help. Open markets where cockroaches crawled across the meat. Pollution. Devastating poverty. Sweltering heat. And so much more. The stress was unbelievable. Resentment and anger welled up inside me toward my husband and toward God. Satan took full advantage of the state of my heart and mind. He had declared war against our family, and I was to be his obvious casualty. A darkness descended upon me, and a deep depression engulfed me. The oppression covering the town blocked out all light and truth in my life. I was drowning, suffocating. I felt trapped. I couldn't function in daily life. I went to bed, and I didn't get up. Thankfully, our field leadership, along with Steve, realized the severity of the situation, and some critical changes were made.

Even though there was some improvement in my mental health, and I managed to survive the remainder of that term, at the end of four years when it was time for our furlough, I was determined that I would never, ever step foot in that country again. However, somehow, a year later, I found myself once more in the Philippines. I continued to struggle during our second term, but when I realized that I was depending more and more on God for strength, constantly quoting the Bible verse: "I can do all things through Christ who gives me strength," it dawned on me that my attitude was slowly changing. The Lord was patiently working in my life. I started to heal and to yield to Him in tiny moment-by-moment steps. There were those times when all I could yield was "willing to be willing" to be in the Philippines. But God knew my heart, and He honored my efforts. My husband lovingly and patiently walked by my side through this challenging season in my life. By the time we returned home for good after 17 years, I had found myself.

Though I'm not sure I would want to re-live those early years on the mission field, I am so very thankful for all that God taught me. He proved Himself over and over to be faithful and trustworthy and strong throughout our four terms of service. There was no way that our mighty God would allow the devil to win the spiritual battle he had waged against us.

The Lord had to take me to the other side of the world to convince me that my security must first come through Him. Steve could not be my savior, and I could not be his rock. Only Jesus was able to rescue me. Only He was capable of giving me the peace, victory, and freedom that I needed. If Christ makes me free, I am free indeed! My guilt is gone. My shame is gone. They have been covered by the blood of Jesus Christ, washing me white as snow. What a tremendous burden was lifted from my heart when I finally accepted all that Christ offers when He extends mercy and forgiveness.

We came away from the Philippines far richer than when we arrived—with a stronger marriage, friendships with Filipinos whom we dearly love, incredible experiences, and a deeper relationship with our Savior.

I do need to be perfectly honest. Even after all I've been through and all I have seen the Lord do, fears and insecurities will pop up out of the blue every now and then. Satan certainly knows my weaknesses and vulnerabilities, and he doesn't hesitate to use them against me. But I catch myself much sooner than I used to. Instead of dwelling on them or allowing them to control my life, I have to stop and deliberately give my fears to the Lord through prayer. I constantly need to be on the alert, guarding my heart and mind in Christ Jesus. For this reason, it's crucial that I spend time reading my Bible, especially the portions that speak to my struggles. One of my favorite Scripture verses says that there is no fear in love because perfect love casts out fear (see 1 John 4:18). Only Jesus is Perfect Love.

As I sat in the grass at the cemetery on that hot, summer day last year, I guess I needed some closure with my dad. I needed to finish my grieving and to let go of what could have been, let go of the opportunities missed, the conversations we never had. I wanted to let him know that I understood about how his life experiences had made him who he was. I so longed to communicate to him what Jesus has done in my life—how He has healed the brokenness and put a soothing balm on my emotional wounds. I wished I'd had the chance to share with Dad about serving the Lord in the very islands where he served his country during World War II, to hear about his experiences in the Philippines and tell him about my adventures there. I wanted to be able to reassure him that I was okay. I hoped my daddy could see his little girl now, all grown up, with a loving husband, four terrific children, three wonderful sons-in-law, and four beautiful grandchildren.

On September 9, 2008, Steve and I celebrated our 36th wedding anniversary. When we walked down the aisle 36 years ago, beginning our new life together, we could never have anticipated what life would hold for us. Yes, many of the years were filled with heartache and struggle. And though the end does not justify the means, God took the hard times, even my sin, and molded us into the people we are today. It continues to amaze me that God would use us, despite ourselves, for the furtherance of His Kingdom. How marvelous is that! The most astonishing wonder has been the security I now feel in Steve's love. As we have grown in our walk with the Lord, we have grown more and more in love with each other. Along with that love, complete trust and respect have been restored. My love for my husband, and his for me, far exceeds anything I could have ever imagined. He is my heart-mate, my soul-mate, my best friend. And we attribute it all to the mercy and grace of our awesome God—and His redeeming love!

My Letters
my heart exposed

November 2003

The Village of Hartville lies south of Akron, Ohio where my husband and I grew up. It has that wonderful small town charm and is surrounded by farmland. It's a lovely area to live, and I am still amazed that God granted me the desires of my heart—a home in "Heart"-ville.

As I drive down the country road, the blazing trees of autumn, with leaves of russet, gold, red, and orange, rustle in the wind. The sky is a startling blue. The sun is shining. The air has just enough nip in it to warrant a sweater. The cornfields are empty as we already enjoyed the harvest of the delicious Ohio sweet corn last month. Pumpkins dot the fields. Roadside stands sell tangy apple cider. Baskets of colorful mums decorate porches. There is even a hint of wood smoke in the air to ward off the chill in someone's home. If you didn't already know that autumn is my favorite season of the year, you surely must know now! It is so beautiful, this corner of my world. It is so beautiful that it makes my heart ache.

How on earth can I feel "pain" from something beautiful? Is it one of those paradoxes of life that doesn't seem to make sense? I realize that one aspect of this feeling is the memories of autumns gone by (my Irish melancholy personality again!). But the flipside of the coin is the joy and delight (ache?) bubbling up inside of me as I take pleasure in the gift that God has given through the season of autumn.

My reflections remind me that I am in the "autumn season" of my life. I'm at the stage where I can relax a bit—I'm not so concerned about making an impression on people or worried about being a "success." I'm comfortable with who I am—sort of like the feeling of wrapping myself in a soft afghan, sipping a cup of hot chocolate, reading a good book. I'm beginning in this season to reap the harvest from my life—and her name is Audrey Paige!

If anything is indicative of pain culminating in beauty, it is new life. Physical birth can be excruciating—especially for the mother, but also for father, baby, and loved ones. I didn't know that it would be so difficult to watch my own daughter labor in the pangs of childbirth! This one who I carried in my womb, close to my heart, and brought into the world in pain, was now striving in pain to bring forth the fruit of her love. As in all instances, I, her mother, wanted to take away her pain. But I've learned over the years that I can't always do that, nor should I, because good comes from the difficult times.

I'm not sure that I can adequately express the emotions of being a grandmother—to see my daughter nurturing her daughter at her breast, gently caressing, gazing at this little one with such intense love. To see a side of my son-in-law that I never saw before as he tenderly holds his daughter, already being fiercely protective. To observe my husband cradle his granddaughter, desiring to give her a godly heritage. To watch my own mother, amazed that she is holding her great-grand-daughter in her arms (four generations of women!). To see my two daughters and my son enthralled with their little niece. And then to hold my granddaughter in my own arms. There are no words. Such love is hard to grasp. Audrey has captured our hearts! The pain was worth it.

Pain begat beauty.

Just as in physical birth, spiritual birth is always a result of suffering. The agony of Christ's death coupled with the anguish of our own souls brings forth something so beautiful, so amazing! New life. Abundant life. Eternal life. There are no words. Such love is hard to grasp. Jesus has captured our hearts!

The cycle of life brings pain and beauty, we can count on it. Whether it be through the seasons of the year or through the seasons of the journey we all must walk, beauty and pain are intertwined.

From Hartville, Ohio, USA, (from my heart) to wherever you are in this world (to your heart), remember that whatever pain you have gone through, or are going through, it will result in indescribable beauty as you reap the harvest of your life when you finally stand before Jesus and hear the words spoken: "Well done, good and faithful servant. Come and share your Master's happiness" (see Matthew 25:21). It will be worth it all!

December 2003

Snow blanketed the earth and covered the trees as we drove down the country road early in the morning. We were headed to Waxhaw, North Carolina, for a "Pastor to Missionaries" conference at the Wycliffe JAARS Center. Christmas lights twinkled on houses as we passed by. Red barns stood in stark contrast against the pristine white snow. All was calm. The countryside was breathtakingly beautiful—a winter wonderland!

Approaching the gently rolling, snow-dusted hills of southern Ohio, "I'll be Home for Christmas" played softly on the radio. It was one of my dad's favorite songs. I can imagine him singing it while stationed in the Pacific during World War II. How many times I sang that same song with tears in my eyes, a lump in my throat, and an ache in my heart, as I'm sure he did. Both of us so far away from home. It's mind-boggling to think that I served the Lord in the very same islands where Dad served his country so many years ago.

> *I'll be home for Christmas*
> *If only in my dreams.*

Christmas must be one of the hardest times for missionaries (and military men/women) to be gone from home—thousands of miles away, with visions of past Christmases dancing in our heads, knowing that loved ones are gathering together without us. So many memories for our hearts to fiercely hold on to.

Having grown up in the Midwest USA, it just didn't seem like Christmas unless we had snow. Trying to conjure up a "white" Christmas in the tropics was a challenge and took a lot of imagination. We could only dream of a white Christmas. However, we did our best. During our second term in the Philippines, we decided to buy an air-conditioner. It was set up in our living room. On Christmas eve, we'd throw our mattresses on the living room floor, turn the air-con on full blast, close the curtains (to pretend it was snowing outside!), turn out the lights and turn on the Christmas lights, wrap ourselves in blankets, drink hot chocolate, and watch the movies *It's a Wonderful Life* and *White Christmas*.

I'm dreaming of a white Christmas, just like the ones I used to know...

I have to admit, it was often difficult to get into the "Christmas spirit" 10,000 miles from home. But I realized that Christmas is Christmas no matter where in the world we are. Jesus came for the whole world, for all people. All Christians observe the coming of the Messiah—we just do it in different ways. Celebrating God's gift of love with our Filipino brothers and sisters was so special. No one celebrates better than Filipinos! The Philippines has the longest Christmas season in the world, starting in September! Remembering Christ's birth together with our friends, singing songs of joy and hope (sung in Tagalog and English), was a small taste of heaven.

Speaking of heaven, lest we forget, Jesus left His home for us. He went from glory to a humble stable. All for me. All for you. Was He ever "homesick"? Maybe spending so many Christmases away from home has made me appreciate even more the sacrifice that He made for us. Of course, it was only the beginning of His suffering, for He was to ultimately go to the cross in payment for our sins. What amazing love! From glory—to a stable—to a cross. But that's not the end of the story, for He will return again, this time in all His glory! What a day that will be! We'll no longer sing, "I'll be home for Christmas, if only in my dreams," for we really will be *home*—home with Jesus, forever!

January 2004

An ice storm has invaded the Midwest. The icy grip of death has invaded our lives. My cousin Sally who has been like a sister to me since childhood, is grieving the death of her father (Butch) and her mother (Betty). On a recent Thursday, I sat in the hospital room with the family as Butch breathed his last breath. Betty, his wife of 62 years, sat by his side and whispered, "I want to go with him." The pain in her eyes and in her voice was hard to bear.

Butch's funeral was on Monday. By evening, Betty had collapsed and was admitted to the hospital. The vigil began. One week to the day of Butch's death, on Thursday, I sat in the hospice room with the family as Betty breathed her last breath. Betty's funeral was on Monday. The whole week had been a sense of *déjà vu*—we've done this before. The family was numb with grief. They had lost father and mother, grandfather and grandmother. Our own hearts were touched with sadness and grief. Betty and Butch had been a part of my life for many years, and I loved them. They surrounded my mom and me with love and care when my dad died in 1968.

In the midst of that week, we attended the funeral of a friend. Wally was one of my husband's first Bible study teachers.

He had struggled with major health issues for 15 years, years that drew him closer to his Shepherd, Jesus. His wife asked Steve to say a few words and pray at the funeral service. Though we knew Wally was safe in the presence of the Lord, the family's grief, as well as our own, tore at our hearts.

Late afternoon on the day of Betty's funeral, I picked Steve up at The Chapel. A winter storm had blown in. Roads were icy and dangerous. An emergency call came through Steve's cell phone. A Chapel family requested the presence of a pastor at their home. Instead of driving to the safety of our home in Hartville, we found ourselves slowly navigating the treacherous roads in the opposite direction. A woman, 47 years old, had been found dead at home by her 19-year-old son. We were smacked in the face once again by grief—witnesses of the misery of a husband and three sons.

Throughout these past two weeks, we have entered into the heartache of family, friends, and strangers—offering prayers for God's comfort, extending love through hugs, sharing sorrow through tears. Today I am emotionally drained. I sit in my rocking chair, safe and warm, staring out the window at the trees glistening with icicles. I want a glimpse of heaven. I need a glimpse of heaven. The lyrics of a song about being in Jesus' presence float into my mind.

I really can only imagine. To be in the presence of awesome majesty and pure love! We carry Him in our hearts here on earth, and He graces us with occasional glimpses of heaven, but to actually be standing, or kneeling, in the presence of Jesus? I can only imagine. I can only imagine the joy when all I will do is forever worship Him!

Joni Eareckson Tada gives us those glimpses that we need from time to time to gain perspective on life. Her book, *Heaven—Your Real Home*, has been recommended to me twice in the past month. Once by a pastor's wife, whose husband battled through cancer. Another time by a dear friend who grieves the death of her granddaughter. What is it that all three of these women, author included, have in common? Heart-wrenching pain. Gut-wrenching grief.

No work today. I don't have the energy. I haven't even changed out of my pajamas. I light a vanilla-scented candle, snuggle down on the couch, and open Joni's book.

March 2004

I lost myself in 1986 when we stepped off the plane onto Philippine soil. Culture shock, inability to speak the language, boarding school, separation, live-in house helper, and much more, stripped me of my identity. I didn't know who I was or who I was supposed to be. I didn't know why I was there.

A caring missionary came alongside of me in the early days. She said, "God has a reason for you to be here. It may not be your reason. It may not be The Chapel's reason. It may not even be SEND International's reason. But God has a purpose for Mary Bucy to be in this country at this time."

What goes through our minds when we think of missions? Naturally, the great commission to go into all the world and preach the gospel, to share Christ and make disciples. But that isn't God's only agenda. A missionary once said, "God has to work on us before He can work through us on the mission field." God took me to the other side of the world, 10,000 miles from home, to work on me and to help me begin the search to find out who I really am.

I am by nature a shy and quiet person, an introvert, with a fearful and Irish melancholic personality. And a pessimist—the cup is always half empty. A bit of a perfectionist, not very flex-ible, impatient.

So God had work to do. And it was painful. He had to strip me bare before He could initiate the rebuilding. Deep depression took hold of my life, forcing us to make some bold changes as a family. Leaving language school and moving to Manila from a provincial town gave me the support I needed and made it possible for our daughters to live at home rather than in the dorm at Faith Academy. Choosing not to have a house helper allowed me to begin to reclaim my "territory." God gave me the freedom to be wife, mother, and homemaker again. I slowly started to heal and to yield to Him in tiny moment-by-moment steps. There were those times when all I could yield was "willing to be willing" to be in the Philippines. But God knew my heart, and He honored my efforts. Through it all, He was faithfully by my side, surrounding me with His grace, lovingly pruning. My husband patiently walked the journey with me.

To our amazement, our honesty about my difficulties began to open doors of friendship and ministry with Filipinos. I wasn't the "holy, bigger-than-life American missionary," but a fellow struggler who could relate to their pain.

While God continued to prune and to use my weaknesses, He began to reveal strengths and characteristics that He had instilled into my life, even using the personality He had created me with. I was still shy, still quiet, still me. He showed me that, instead of changing me into an extrovert, He could take an introvert and use me for His purposes.

The Lord unwrapped the gift of mercy in me—a tender and caring heart that hurt with others, with the desire to encourage and help. He put thoughts into my head and heart that had to be written down. He took a wife's heart, a mother's heart, a daughter's heart, a friend's heart, and allowed me to minister to wives and mothers and daughters and friends, both Filipinas and expat missionaries, through my journal writings. My honesty and vulnerability helped other women to be honest in looking at their own lives. By giving them access to my life, they in turn ministered to me by sharing their lives. And I am the richer for it.

There were times that I stepped out of my comfort zone, only to find that I am not a teacher, I am not a speaker, I am not an evangelist. I am an ordinary woman who wants to serve Christ. And He gave me the incredible privilege, with my family, to do just that for 17 years in the Philippines. And along the way, I found myself.

April 2004

Signs of spring surround me. Sounds of excitement escape my lips as I spot the first robin of the season. Joy bubbles up inside when I discover tiny buds on the forsythia bushes in my backyard and as I look upon the crocuses and daffodils pushing up through the soil. Pleasure is seen on my face as I awaken to the twittering of birds in the tree outside my bedroom window. Even the rain, rain, rain does not dampen my spirits as I anticipate the world blooming around me. I haven't experienced spring for five years!

Probably one of the most significant signs of spring for Akronites is the opening of Strickland's Frozen Custard stand. I remember our former pastor saying that the ice cream must be sinful since it is so good! Strickland's is definitely an icon in the area. There was an article in the newspaper recently, telling of a transplanted Akronite in California opening a franchise of Strickland's. You'll never guess who her first customer was—another transplanted Akronite! Strickland's invokes happy memories for many who have called Akron, and the surrounding areas, home.

Did I say spring is in the air? Yeah, right! Today is April first, and Mother Nature has pulled a fast one on us. Her idea of an April Fool's joke is *snow*! Spring is fickle in Northeast Ohio. We can experience all four seasons in one day!

I remember spring down south when we lived in Columbia, South Carolina. It arrives much earlier than it does up north.

The world was literally bursting with color! The azalea bushes seemed to be on fire. The fragrance of the magnolias was intoxicating.

Another sure sign of spring in the U.S. is the cherry blossoms. My daughters Hester and Ruthanne, granddaughter Audrey, and I visited with my daughter Sarah and son-in-law Brandon in Virginia on a beautiful weekend. They graciously put us up in their small apartment, fed us (Brandon is a wonderful cook!), and took us into Washington D.C. on the metro to view the famous Cherry Blossoms, Japan's gift to the U.S. The trees were absolutely gorgeous, with various shades of pink and white. We have some terrific pictures of the Jefferson Memorial and the Washington Monument framed with cherry blossoms.

I think I must love all the seasons. It's one of the things I missed most when living in the tropics—the four seasons of Ohio! In the Philippines, we had two seasons—hot and wet and hot and dry! Although autumn is my absolute favorite, after a long, cold winter, I'm so glad springtime is just around the corner. People will begin flocking to Cuyahoga Valley to view the return of the herons. It's quite an amazing sight to see the babies' heads popping out of the nests up in the trees and to watch the herons swooping down in the marshy areas or soaring in the sky. The clocks will "spring" ahead soon, and we will have more daylight. Everything "springs" to life after a period of dormancy.

Even people tend to hibernate through the winter months, so when the sun shines warmly on my face, I feel alive and full of energy. My energy, naturally, turns to our house. The spring cleaning bug has bitten me! I want to throw open the windows and let a gentle wind blow through the house. I want to shake out the dust from the rugs and wipe the cobwebs off the ceilings and wash the windows. A clean house feels so good. The yard needs tending, too. Twigs off the trees are scattered around, remnants of winter storms. Dead plants that didn't get taken care of in the fall need to be weeded out. The grass needs cutting, the bushes need trimming. Even the cars need to have the salt from the winter roads washed off.

After being shut up inside for most of the winter, I will finally get to stroll through my new neighborhood, getting better acquainted with neighbors who we briefly met last September when we moved in. I can't wait to take my granddaughter for a walk in her stroller. It will be so fun to see her reactions to the great big world outside—a whole new world for her. Besides, walking gives me much needed exercise after inactivity through the winter months.

The frozen earth is being renewed, the house is getting cleaned. Perhaps I need a bit of inner spring cleaning as well. I feel the need to dust off the cobwebs of my mind, examine my heart, replenish my soul. Everyone has been talking about the book *The Purpose Driven Life* by Rick Warren. It has even penetrated the lives of our Filipino friends on the other side of the world. This seems like just the prescription for me.

Although I'm not very far into the book, I love how the author thinks. He tells us that God gains pleasure as He watches us enjoy His creation.

I have to smile because I imagine God smiling and taking great delight in knowing that He has brought pleasure to me through the miracle of spring. Maybe He really did laugh with joy at my excitement when I saw the first robin of the season. What a fantastic feeling to know that I can bring pleasure to my Lord by simply enjoying His gift of springtime. And in so doing, I worship Him, the Author of life. Doesn't that just make your heart burst with love for Him! Happy spring!

May 2004

I went to the cemetery today—Holy Cross Cemetery. We buried my grandmother there when I was nine and my dad when

I was 17. My cousin Sally's parents were buried there this past January. So many lie beneath the ground—great-grandparents, aunts, uncles, cousins. How many funerals did I attend, and how many tears were shed in that place?

A sob caught in my throat when I visited the grave of my best friend from high school days. I wasn't home for her funeral last year. Maybe that's why at times it still seems so unreal. Seeing Sherry's name engraved on the stone, though, made me confront reality, and a fresh wave of sorrow washed over me. A piece of my heart, a piece of my past, was buried with her.

The cemetery is located in the Firestone Park area of Akron, where I grew up. So when I drive out, I am instantly transported back to my teen years and memories of Sherry. Garfield High School. Hi Teens. LuJann's Drive-in. Cruising down Kenmore Boulevard. Football games at the Rubber Bowl. Steve. Yes, Steve! Sherry was as excited as I was when Steve walked me home from Hi Teens. Sher was a great friend and a fun person. I can't count the times I've wanted to pick up the phone and talk to her. I really miss her.

As I drove through "The Park," remnants of the past flooded my thoughts. There were so many wonderful memories. But there were some difficult ones as well. Sure, we had the normal teenage issues, but we also had some big crises come into our young lives. Sherry had complications from diabetes—the very disease that eventually claimed her life. It's a scary thing to see your friend on the edge of a diabetic coma. Death shouldn't be something that we had to deal with, and yet it seemed a very real possibility as we rushed Sherry to the hospital. And then my dad suffered through a painful bout of cancer and died the summer between my junior and senior years of high school, in 1968. Death was personal. Tragedy had struck home.

I experienced another death that summer of 1968—a "spiritual death." I turned my back on God. In my selfish thinking, He had turned His back on me when He didn't answer my prayers for Dad's healing. My limited knowledge of God's character could not see how He could allow such agony. My finite understanding of God could not see how He could cause good to come from Dad's death.

It's horrendous and frightening to be in a spiritual limbo. It was eight long years. And then He did use it for good in my life and brought me out of darkness into His marvelous light! But even though I had given my life to Christ, the struggles and fears did not vanish instantly. If I were to be honest, I'd have to admit that there are still gray days. This was most evident in our early months in the Philippines. We had moved to a provincial town to attend language school. Baliwag was an oppressive place, a spiritual stronghold dedicated to the image of the Santo Nino (Christ Child). Several missionaries had had to leave town for various reasons—health, family-related, mental, spiritual, marital. Our mission organization was in the early stages of planting a church. Spiritual warfare pervaded the town. A black cloud hovered over, blocking out light and truth. And it affected me. A deep depression took hold of my life. The aftereffects lingered even to the point that, as much as possible, I avoided returning to Baliwag for any reason. I think it was at the end of our second term, while visiting another missionary there, that I realized that I had to "face" my past. I literally walked through the town praying and exorcising my personal "demons."

As I grow in my walk with the Lord, the fears and darkness have gradually diminished to mere shadows. Perhaps the shadows will not completely fade away until I stand in the presence of the Light. But until that day, I am encouraged in knowing that His Holy Spirit is with me now, in the present, and will be with me in my future.

What of my past? Was He there? As the memories tumble around in my mind, I have to acknowledge that He indeed was there. Do you know what a comfort that is to my heart? To know that *Jesus was in my past*? Always faithful, always involved, always caring, always loving. He knew everything about me. He knew me before I was a twinkle in my parents' eyes. He knit me together in my mother's womb. He wanted me to be born with dark hair and brown eyes on July 28, 1951, in Akron, Ohio, to Leroy and Anna McDermott. He wanted me to be an only child. He wanted me to be friends with Sherry, to meet Steve and fall in love with him.

He was always there. In the depths of despair? He was there. At the height of excitement? He was there. He knew every painful trial and every moment of celebration—every big and small detail of what was going on in my life. He was there when Dad's casket was lowered into the ground. He was there when I married my high school sweetheart. He was there through the fears and when the darkness was so thick it didn't seem that any light could penetrate it. In all of life's low valleys and high mountaintops, even though I refused to see Him, He was there. Jesus was *always* right where He *said* He would be.

June 2004

"Oh, Mary, you have a small treasure here!" Those were the words that my friend Marcia exclaimed as she discovered Lily of the Valley tucked away on the side of the house. Since I have not had much experience with gardening, I asked Marcia to come over and help me identify everything growing in my yard. I grew some gorgeous marigolds at our first house in the mid-70s. I even tried to grow marigolds in the Philippines, but I didn't have any success. They just wouldn't take root in the soil. So you can see how limited my knowledge of gardening is!

As we continued to walk around the yard, Marcia's excitement grew contagious. I was catching her enthusiasm! There were chives, mint, oregano, parsley, sage, rhubarb, daisies, peonies, hydrangea, iris, primrose, hyacinth, bleeding heart, yarrow, rhododendron, azaleas, lilacs. Wow! The ladies we bought the house from really did leave us a treasure!

Just as Marcia and I walked around the outside of the house searching for treasure, I later found myself walking around the inside of the house searching for treasure that is close to my heart.... Dad's sweater. The American flag that draped his casket. The heart-shaped pin from Mom with my name on it. My grandmother's bracelet that my dad made for her from Australian coins during World War II. The pearl and onyx ring that Steve bought me after high school graduation. The afghan my mother-in-law crocheted for us. The picture frame from my daughter Sarah with the words "World's Best Mom" and a picture of her and me sleeping on the couch when she was a small child. The jewelry box my daughter Ruthanne made for me in high school woodshop. The Willow Tree plaque with a mother holding her child that my daughter Hester gave me. The heart-shaped rock my son Micah found for me on a beach in the Philippines. The Hartville Chocolate Factory sweatshirt that my friend Joan bought for me one birthday while we were spending time together visiting all the charming shops in Hartville. (Little did we know that one day Hartville would be home!) Baby booties that my friend Sherry brought back from Italy. The cross-stitched Precious Moments picture with the words "You have touched so many hearts" from the Homebuilders ABF ladies. It started my collection of hearts! The "Bless your heart" pillow from my Filipina friends. Anne Morrow Lindbergh's book *Gift from the Sea* from my friend Sally. The little silver heart that my friend Natsuko brought me from Japan. The cross-stitched "A friend loves at all times" from my friend Felicia. The scrapbook that the SEND ladies made for me before we left the Philippines last year. The many pictures of family and friends on tables, fireplace mantles, walls, and so much more. Precious objects full of lovely memories.

But they are just that—objects. It's what, or rather, who they represent that is the real treasure—the people I cherish, the relationships that make up the tapestry of my life. "When someone you love becomes a memory, the memory becomes a treasure." These words, framed by a heart-shaped wreath of flowers, hang on the wall surrounded by pictures of loved ones no longer here. As I indulged in a bit of reminiscence, a melancholy sigh escaped my lips. Then I moved on to pictures of the living. Baby pictures. Graduation pictures. Wedding pictures.

My gaze lingered on one particular frame. The words "A Circle of Friends" are encircled with eight small pictures. I saw myself at the top. The other seven openings hold pictures of seven very special women in my life—women who prayed me back to the Philippines for a fourth term when all I wanted to do was stay home. They saw me at my ugliest, and yet they still loved me and cared enough to pray for me to be willing to do what God wanted me to do, even if that meant leaving my three daughters behind in the States. Their prayers didn't stop there. They prayed me through the next four years. They prayed for God's perfect peace. They prayed that God would use me. They prayed that we would end well. And then they prayed me back home again.

God honored the prayers of these godly women. He gave me His peace, even in the midst of separation. I believe He used me in the lives of other women. And we ended our missionary service well. It was a most amazing four years—years that I would have missed if seven wonderful women had not been loving enough to embrace, compassionate enough to cry, brave enough to confront, bold enough to gently push, and caring enough to pray.

When you go into a Hallmark store, you can often find cards that liken friends to bouquets of flowers. My yard is blooming with beautiful flowers. My heart is blooming with beautiful friends.

Thank you, Sharon, Lori, Linda, Marcia, Margo, Karen, and Mary. You are treasures!

July 2004

"You Were Shaped to Serve God." This is probably my favorite chapter in *The Purpose Driven Life*.

The author, Rick Warren, tells us that God does not waste anything that happens in our lives. Everything happens for a reason. God uses all of our experiences to mold us to serve Him and minister to others. He uses the abilities and personalities He gave us to bring glory to Himself.

These are liberating statements! I'm free to be me! For someone who has struggled with low self-esteem and envy, this is significant. It's true that I "found myself" in the Philippines, and I've grown more comfortable in my skin, but occasionally, issues will pop up, seemingly out of nowhere. I wish I could sing like her. Or I wish I could be bold enough to share Christ like her... or cook like her... or paint like her. But God did not intend for me to have those abilities or gifts, so those thoughts have to be squelched immediately.

Mr. Warren goes on to say that we are uniquely designed by God. He has a purpose for our lives, a role planned for each of us. As I continued reading, the author seemed to be saying that if we don't fulfill our purpose, contributing our part, then no one else will fill that role. Wow, that's powerful and thought-provoking!

We had friends over for dinner yesterday. Our conversation turned to the topic of not letting "divine" situations slip by us. Ted said something to the effect that God knows that a certain person in your life (friend, co-worker, neighbor, whoever) is going to come to Christ. He wants to use you. But if you pass up the opportunity, He'll use someone else. We are regular people who work regular jobs, live regular lives, but are rubbing shoulders with unbelievers. We are the only Bible some people ever come in contact with. We are the only church many people will ever be involved with. Ted and Karen used this as a challenge recently to their peers in Homebuilders ABF. They said that those of us in this stage of life (50s) tend to think that we've raised our children, so we can relax a bit now and kind of cruise through the rest of our lives.

I'm ashamed to admit that I've sort of had this mindset. Sometimes this thought flitters through my mind: "*Okay, Lord, I've done my duty serving you as a missionary in the Philippines. Now I can just relax and enjoy life in the U.S.*" I don't think that sits too well with the Lord. And really, it doesn't sit too well with me either, especially after hearing what Ted and Karen had to say and reading what Rick Warren wrote. I don't want to pass up the opportunities that God brings my way. How sad it must make Him when we don't take advantage of the gifts, time, abilities, money, and experiences that He has given us to minister His love and compassion to others, and in so doing, bring glory to Him. I don't have a beautiful singing voice or the gift of hospitality or teaching abilities. But this should not prevent me from reaching out to others. Instead, I should take how He has shaped me and use the gifts He has given me to touch another life.

When I look inside my heart, as Mr. Warren seems to suggest we do, I find a passion, an emotional heartbeat, to encourage women: Through my writing. Through my prayers. Through my friendship. With a comforting word, a thoughtful act, a gentle touch, a tender embrace, a compassionate mercy. Being knit together in love means that I weep with, rejoice with, celebrate with, laugh with.

The Lord has brought women into my life for this time and this season. I want Him to use me to minister grace to their lives and to let them know what Christ has done for me so that they may find peace for their hearts and assurance of salvation. I dare not turn away from this "divine" door that God has opened. A life depends on it. A soul could be lost for eternity.

Besides, I don't want to miss the chance to store up treasures in heaven and add a jewel to my crown—the very crown that I will one day lay at the feet of my Savior in gratitude and love and praise! I don't know about you, but when I stand before Jesus, I don't want to see sadness in His eyes. What I want to see is a twinkle of pride as He says the words we all long to hear, "Great job, my good and faithful servant."

August 2004

The end of summer is fast approaching. Autumn will soon find me in my garden—on my knees. I am determined not to make the same mistake I made last year. I suffered the consequences of my lack of discipline in weeding, pruning, and cleaning the flower beds last September. It doesn't matter that I was exhausted from scraping wallpaper, painting, and moving into our house. Mother Nature was not sympathetic toward my plight.

As the flowers started to bloom this spring, and as the rain continued to fall, I realized the error of my ways. Lying hidden beneath these "treasures" were dead, decaying leaves, vines tangling around the plants, slimy slugs, and other equally disgusting things. Long, hard work was required to clean this up. With aching back, scratched arms, and dirty fingernails, I wondered how anyone could say that you are "closer to God in a garden than anywhere else on earth"! This was ugly and dirty, not to mention, painful. On the surface, the flowers were beautiful. But underneath? Yuck!

Sounds a bit like my life—before Christ. When I was not living in the light of Christ's love, ugly, slimy sin was uncovered in the darkness of my heart. Even now, as a child of God, the world encroaches with overgrown and tangled vines that want to choke the life out of me. Weeds (thoughts, attitudes, motives, selfishness, pride, whatever) creep in, and if I don't quickly pull them up, they threaten to overtake and affect my relationships and my testimony.

Weeds in life, just like the weeds in my garden, are sometimes deceptive. As my friend Marcia and I walked around my yard, I pointed and said, "Oh, that's pretty." "That's a weed, Mary," Marcia answered in a serious tone. There's much out there in the world that looks pretty or feels good. How blessed we are if there is someone who cares enough to tell us that the enticing thing is harmful and nothing but a weed that will prevent growth in our lives. We ourselves need to be on our knees praying for protection, wisdom, and discernment.

It's not just the weeds, though, and this is where life gets confusing. Marcia told me that I needed to regularly trim back the plants, some of them almost to the ground. To cut back the beautiful plants seemed brutal! These are good plants, not harmful weeds. But she assured me that it was necessary if I wanted lush foliage and longer lasting blooms. Sometimes we need to cut back or trim seemingly worthwhile activities. Forego that church function to spend time with our kids. Miss that meeting to take an elderly parent to the doctor. Decide not to attend one more Bible study, and instead, minister to a hurting friend. Make the choice not to go to another marriage seminar, and choose to do something fun with our husbands. Skip that conference, and use the quiet time for ourselves. All these activities can be beneficial, so how can they also be detrimental? They can be harmful if they hurt our health, rob us of moments with loved ones, prevent us from reaching out, or keep us from time with our Lord.

Gardening is hard work. There's no getting around that, unless I hire someone to do the work for me. But then the garden wouldn't seem that it was really mine, because I did not cultivate it. For it to be my garden, my own personal time, discipline, commitment, and consistency are required. That's not to say that I can't have help. Marcia pulled weeds and planted pansies. My daughter Hester pulled weeds. My husband Steve and son Micah cut the grass, moved rocks, and pounded stakes into the ground under my direction. But I wasn't just supervising, I was working, too. Now when I sit on my screened-in porch, I can see the results, the fruits of my labor. There is a joy and contentment that comes from creating. You should have seen my excitement when I held my first red, sun-ripened tomato in my hand! The thrill I get from the beauty of the flowers and the birds that are attracted to my yard are rewards for a job well done.

A life lived for Christ is hard work. There's no getting around that. It requires time, discipline, commitment, and consistency. The Lord's weeding and pruning can be painful. The result, though, is a life of beauty, not just on the surface, but underneath as well. The life that is cultivated with the help of the Holy Spirit is surely one that will be attractive to others and that will reap great rewards.

Yes, autumn will find me on my knees in my garden. On my knees—not a bad place to be.

October 2004

Thirty-eight Septembers ago, a cute, blond-haired, blue-eyed, 15-year-old boy walked a shy, dark-haired, brown-eyed, 15-year-old girl home from a Hi-Teens dance.

Thirty-two Septembers ago, the boy married the girl...and they lived happily ever after.

The...dots...between "married" and "ever after" depict an amazing story of grace. It's a story of love and tears and pain and forgiveness and salvation and joy. It's my story. It's Steve's story. It's *our* story!

We celebrated our story this year on Wednesday, September 8, the day before our wedding anniversary. It was Steve's regular day off from work, which allowed us to spend the whole day together. Dancing in the privacy of our home to our song, "When a Man Loves a Woman" by Percy Sledge, the years slipped away, if only for a few moments, and we were teenagers again. It was just the two of us throughout the day, remembering, reflecting on all the different paths we have walked together over the years. Ten years (four married) without Christ. Twenty-eight with Him. Jesus changed our lives, and we are forever grateful. Later in the evening, we finished the wonderful day with a delicious dinner at Carrabas Italian Restaurant.

Every now and then, I catch glimpses of that 15-year-old boy. But I love the man that Steve has become—a man after God's own heart. He is a man of prayer. First Thessalonians 5:17 says that we should "pray without ceasing." This describes Steve, and his life reflects it. He is a man who treasures the Word of God. You can see it by the look of delight on his face and hear it from the excitement in his voice when he reads Scripture from the pulpit or when he teaches a class or when he preaches. He is a man who truly loves the Lord. His life testifies to it.

I not only love the man that Steve has become, but also I am proud of the man he has become. He is a man of integrity, a man of peace, a man of grace. And he has such a tender heart for people. The Lord has divinely imparted pastoral gifts to him. This is obvious to all as he ministers care and compassion with humility.

As a husband, the Lord must have known that Steve was the only one for me. He's loving, gentle, strong, and patient. He's not perfect. He has weaknesses and faults like everyone, but this doesn't diminish him in my sight. I love him all the more. I cherish our time together—whether it's doing something fun or having a serious conversation or sitting together in silence.

As his wife, I feel such a calming sense of security in his arms. He's my best friend, my heart-mate, and I'm so very thankful for the deep love that we share.

Steve is a fantastic father. Sarah, Ruthanne, Hester, and Micah would attest to this. In fact, he helped me to see what our Heavenly Father is like through his own example with our children. He's a wonderful grandfather, and this will become more evident as Audrey gets older and as other grandchildren are born into our family.

I am filled with wonder as I look back over our 38 years together, from teenagers to middle-agers! There were some mighty rough bumps in our road, but by the grace of God, we stuck with it and worked through the tough times. Instead of tearing us apart, the challenges we faced deepened our commitment to each other. We've grown in countless ways together and have had some extraordinarily exciting and unusual experiences, especially during our years in the Philippines. Life is never dull with Steve!

Thirty-eight years! Where has the time gone? It sounds like an eon ago, and yet it seems like only yesterday.

Even though almost four decades have passed since I first fell hopelessly in love with him, Steve can still make my heart flutter when he looks at me with those baby blue eyes! Just like he did when we were 15.

November 2004

October was a month of many moods. Autumn always puts me in a melancholy, pensive mood anyway, even as I'm reveling in God's colorful palette brushed across the trees. So many wonderful things happened during the month that I am puzzled at the contrasting moods of happiness and sadness I experienced over events that were good and right.

My granddaughter Audrey turned one on October 6, moving on to toddlerhood. The day before, on October 5, my own "baby," Micah, turned 20, leaving his teenage years behind. My daughter Hester celebrated her 25th birthday on October 10, the same day we had Audrey's birthday party at our house. That evening, Hester moved out to share an apartment with two friends. She's been on her own before, having studied at Messiah College in Pennsylvania for four years. Moving out is a good thing for her, but it brought sadness to my heart. I liked having her around. After college graduation, she came out to the Philippines where she was with us for our last year in the country. She tends to be Asian "by heart," so this was a positive experience for her. She took linguistics classes toward her master's degree at a seminary in Manila, and then helped with the new TESOL program that our mission started. When Steve, Micah, and I returned to Ohio at the end of May 2003, Hester returned with us. She was a tremendous help when we moved into our house in September of last year. She did most of the painting! What a gift to have her with us for these past two years. Even though she didn't move very far away, it was still hard to see her go. Thankfully, my daughter Sarah was in town from Virginia for Audrey's birthday party. She cushioned the transition for us, even if only for one night. But then, after making her chocolate chip pancakes for breakfast the next morning, I had to say goodbye. There was a lump in my throat as I waved, watching her car disappear down the street. How I long for the day when there will be no more goodbyes!

It's a bit weird for Steve and me, having an empty nest. For the first time in 31 years, it's just the two of us. Of course, Micah will be home from Wheaton College for breaks and for the summers. But it's not quite the same. We have moved on to a new season of life. This season, as I've shared before, has brought the blessing of being grandparents. Shortly after our last child left for his first year of college, little Audrey came into our lives. What a delight she has been, taking away a bit of the ache of sending our youngest out into the world. God amazes us with His timing.

And He continues to amaze. Next summer, Audrey will have a little cousin to play with, and we will have another bundle of joy added to our family. Yes, Sarah is pregnant! I'm allowed to share the news now. She and Brandon will become parents in June, 2005. To say I am thrilled is an understatement! I found out the day of Audrey's birthday party. She had just finished opening her presents. Ruthanne, Audrey's mom and my daughter, said, "There is one more present...for Grandma, to thank her for letting us have the party at her house." She handed it to Audrey, who then handed it to me. There was a beautiful picture frame inside the box with the words: "Grandma, we love you." I thanked them. Ruthanne asked me to read the words out loud, which I did. She then said, "Read it again, Mom. It says *we* love you." "That's so sweet," I said, thinking that she meant that Audrey *and* Ruthanne and Ryan loved me. Ruthie continued, "Mom, you're not getting it." I looked at her with a startled expression on my face and asked, "Are you pregnant?" "No, Mom." It was so quiet in the room you could have heard a pin drop. And then it dawned on me. I looked at Sarah, who was sitting on the floor next to me, and exclaimed with a question, "Is Sarah pregnant?" And then pandemonium broke loose as everyone screamed and cried and hugged. Poor little Audrey got scared from all the noise and started to cry too. What a dramatic and fun way they chose to tell me! When things settled down, I talked to my son-in-law on the phone. He was not able to get away from work, so Sarah had made the trip by herself. I saw him a couple of weeks later, when we traveled down to Virginia to help him celebrate his 30th birthday, and was then able to give him a big hug.

I've teased both Sarah and Brandon that they are breaking with tradition. All the kids have October or November birthdays: Hester, Micah, and Audrey in October, and Sarah, Brandon, Ruthanne, and Ryan in November. Although now that I think of it, a summer baby will be most welcome, as Steve's birthday is in June and mine is in July.

As you can see, October obviously was a month of many moods. Even though I don't understand how my emotions can roller-coaster from happy to sad all in one breath, I do know that my heart is so full right now that it feels like it could burst with the wonder of it all. As Micah said when Sarah called him with the good news, "Oh happy days!"

P.S. Just as I was finishing up this letter, I received a telephone call from Ruthanne. Not only will Audrey have a new cousin next summer, she'll also have a new baby brother or sister in July! Oh happy days, indeed!

December 2004

"Queen Mary!" That's what was written on the card in front of me at the table when my prayer circle gathered together last July at my friend Marcia's house to celebrate my birthday. What a treat for me! As you can imagine, **Marcia** has the ability to make a person feel special. She is a gracious hostess. She has such a tender heart. She's a wonderful cook, has a lovely home, and attends to the smallest detail. I've witnessed this, as well as experienced it, many times. She has the gift of hospitality.

While recently pondering this concept of hospitality, which we are all to be practicing, even if it's not our gift, I came to the conclusion that it can manifest itself in a variety of ways, with each individual giving it his or her own personal spin.

Ronnie built a charming English cottage with the intent of running a bed and breakfast. Zoning laws prohibited this venture, but this did not dampen Ronnie's enthusiasm. She has used her home countless times to minister to people, myself included. She loves to pamper, and she does it well with her delicious meals, cozy house, attractive yard, comfy beds, and bubbly personality.

World Changers (a group of missionaries, parents of missionaries, and those interested in missions) meets once a month. **Billee** and **Janis** have both hosted our times of potluck, fellowship, and prayer in their homes. They and their husbands have often graciously housed missionaries who were home from the field.

Sharon sheltered me on several occasions over the years when I made trips home alone from the Philippines to spend time with my daughters. Sharon is a nurse, and since she works outside of the home at a local hospital, she would hand me a house key, allowing me to come and go as I pleased, even loaning me her car. She gave me the freedom to do what I came home to do—spend time with my girls. We usually had dinner together a few times to talk and catch up on our lives. Not only has her home been a haven for me, but also Sharon is a safe friend. I always feel comfortable in her home.

Joan, along with her family, opened their home and hearts to our two oldest daughters when they returned to the States to attend college. I found this verse in Psalm 68 when Sarah first left the Philippines: "He places the lonely in families" (see Psalm 68:6). Next to that verse, in the margin of my Bible, I wrote "MKs" (missionary kids). Sarah and Ruthanne fall under that category of MKs, and God answered our prayers by placing them in a family. Being separated from them perpetuated a constant ache in my heart, but I knew that I left them in the care of the person who was like a sister to me. The Davies made it possible for us to continue our ministry in the Philippines, knowing that our girls were watched over by friends who had the same values and beliefs that we did. It wasn't always easy, could at times be quite difficult, blending two families—different personalities, different ways of doing things. It was often a challenge for all, but this family believed their house was the Lord's and felt He would have them do this as a ministry. I know my girls learned much from Joan. She's a fantastic cook. Not only does she have the gift of hospitality, but also she has a real knack for organization. Her house is always clean and organized.

Not only did Joan and her family open their home to our daughters, but also there were several times that our whole family stayed with them. And I can't even count the times that

I found myself under the shelter of their roof. One particular time comes to mind. I was in town for Ruthanne's college graduation. Wanting to say goodnight to everyone, I ran down the carpeted steps in my stocking feet. Not a good combination where I am concerned! I fell and severely broke my left ankle. Joan rushed me to the hospital and stayed with me until I was admitted hours later. After surgery and a few days in the hospital, I found myself on Joan's couch. She fixed my meals, washed my hair, and helped me with whatever needed to be done. There's no doubt in my mind that I tested her patience with my demands or my crankiness from being stuck in the house. But she continued to serve me, going the extra mile. I could never repay Joan for all she has done for our family over the years. I know a wonderful reward awaits her in heaven.

Filipinos seem to have a corner on the market of hospitality. How often we were recipients of their warmth and friendliness. Their willingness to share their best, even when other family members went without, was humbling. I remember distinctly one of the most pleasant and relaxing evenings I ever spent in the Philippines. **Mimi** and Rodel are a middle-class, professional couple. They had just bought a piece of property on the outskirts of Metro Manila. A bahay kubo (small shelter made from palms) was erected on the lot temporarily until they were able to construct a house. The yard was already beautifully landscaped. We were just days away from departing from what we thought would be our last term of service in their country (we actually ended up returning for one more term), and they invited us over to say goodbye. A table was set up out in the open, under the stars. Since we were on the fringe of the city, we were not plagued with pollution and noise. Music played softly in the background. Mimi prepared a delicious meal of pancit (noodle dish that she knew was my favorite), bangus (stuffed fish that she knew was Steve's favorite), rice, and fresh tropical fruits. What a delightful time we had with these dear friends!

Speaking of the Philippines, I can't forget to mention our **SEND Guest House**. This is a ministry that definitely requires a heart of hospitality. We stayed at the GH several times over our years in the Philippines, and we saw a variety of managers come and go. Each added a unique "flavor" to this vital ministry. **Linda** (and her husband Frank) brought a Midwest USA flavor, along with her wisdom from life experiences. **Nancy** brought a Southern USA flavor, along with her friendliness and exuberance. She loves the adventure of discovering and exploring places in and around Manila. Others brought flavors of Germany or Canada. They ministered not only to the SEND missionaries, but also to people from many different nations who were in the country for assorted reasons.

As with any other spiritual gift that the Lord bestows on His children, the woman who possesses the gift of hospitality adds her own personality, strengths, experiences, and talents. It's been fun and exciting for me to see each of my friends' willingness to extend God's love, grace, and care in her own unique way. Their ministry to me has not only met my physical needs, but also my heart needs as well. And I have indeed been blessed!

February 2005

I'm a hopeless romantic. Just ask my husband. There's nothing I enjoy more than a good love story. I have had the incredible privilege, over the past several months, to be an eyewitness of a true love story.

We've known Jerry and Dorla for just a short time. Though they were part of our ABF (Sunday school class), it wasn't until we started sitting behind them in the sanctuary during worship service that the Lord began to give me glimpses of their love. As Sunday after Sunday passed, I caught small gestures of love as Dorla placed her hand on Jerry's arm or lay her head on his shoulder. There were moments when I observed the tears of a wife overcome with the emotions of love and pain and fear. My heart continually ached for Dorla, until one Sunday I sensed the Lord prompting me to do something more than say "good morning" or "I'm praying for you." The something I wanted to do was take away her pain, but I knew I couldn't. What I could do was help her carry it. And so I laid my hand on her shoulder to let her know I was there to walk with her through the tough road ahead. This was the beginning of a relationship that only God in His sovereignty could orchestrate. If I had the time, I'd tell you all the reasons why, but I'd rather tell you what I witnessed over the past few months.

As we sat in hospital rooms and hospital waiting rooms, Steve and I had the opportunity to get to know Jerry and Dorla. And Dorla allowed me occasional glimpses into her heart as she spoke of the tall, strong, and handsome man who captured her heart more than 40 years ago.

We saw a deep and unconditional love that Jerry and Dorla shared for each other and for their Lord. We observed a strong commitment and an even stronger faith. Even when the days were difficult and the pain was overwhelming, their love and their faith did not waver. They fought courageously for life, valiantly for love.

The last expression of love that I personally witnessed between Jerry and Dorla will forever be etched in my mind. I stood in the room at the Aultman Woodlawn care facility. Jerry was heavily sedated, and his eyelids were half closed. Dorla lay on the bed next to him, caressing his forehead with her hand and whispering in his ear. It was such a private, intimate moment that I felt I should look away. But I was mesmerized by the depth of love this woman had for her husband. I remember hoping that he was aware of her presence. And then he turned his head and moved his cheek closer to her. That simple, tender gesture spoke volumes and I knew this man cherished his wife and she was the reason he fought so hard to live.

They say that one of the greatest gifts a father can give his children is to love their mother. Jerry gave his son and daughter a wonderful gift.

I'm so grateful the Lord allowed our paths to cross with Jerry and Dorla. His intentions were more than just my reaching out to a hurting sister. He wanted me to be an eyewitness of a true love story.

The Lord called Jerry home to heaven in January, after a two-year battle with pancreatic cancer. And so today, I celebrate the love that Dorla and Jerry shared. A love that I know will live on in her heart until that day she stands together with him, in awe, in the very presence of the Holy One who blessed them with such an amazing love.

March 2005

The luxury of a whole day at home—with the house all to myself! It wasn't actually a choice that I made voluntarily, though. After all, there are always places to go and things to do. With one car down, my husband Steve needed the other one for work. Without transportation, I was "stuck" at home. Instead of seeing it as an inconvenience, I chose to welcome it as a gift.

There was nothing pressing to be done. The laundry was caught up. The house was tidy. It was not yet the season for major spring cleaning projects. Gloomy winter skies still hovered over Northeast Ohio. Turning on the television for a bit of company, I found black-and-white Andy Griffith show reruns. Time spent with Andy, Barney, Opie, and Aunt Bee is always time well spent for me. Indulging in an hour of the show proved therapeutic. Barney never fails me. His antics produce light-hearted laughter, no matter what's going on in my life.

And there is something going on. A dark cloud is hanging over our family. My stepfather Paul has recently been diagnosed with cancer of the esophagus. The road ahead is uncertain, most likely a long and difficult one. I worry about my mom. She went through this with my dad 38 years ago. Remembering vividly his pain, as well as her own, gives birth to fear and anxiety in her heart. Will God give her the grace and strength to endure this again? Of course He will! And we are here to share the burden with her and with Paul.

The journey Paul will be walking will be a painful one. We hate to see loved ones face physical suffering, and yet we know that with cancer this is inevitable. Feeling helpless, we pray, but not as a last resort. Instinctively, it's the first thing we want to do, to take our cares to a loving and compassionate Father, knowing that He will listen, and He will respond.

Laughing through the Andy Griffith show released the tightness in my chest. Sitting at the kitchen table later, watching the birds at the feeders in my yard, suppressed the churning of my stomach. Watering the plants brought a sense of normalcy. Finally, succumbing to tears released pent-up emotions. Reading the Bible calmed my anxious spirit. It just so happened that my quiet time with the Lord found me in the book of Philippians, one of my favorite portions of Scripture. Chapter four, verses four, six, and seven, says: "Rejoice in the Lord always. I will say it again: Rejoice!... Do not be anxious about anything, but in everything, by prayer and petition, with thanksgiving, present your requests to God. And the peace of God, which transcends all understanding, will guard your hearts and your minds in Christ Jesus." Presenting my requests to God did bring peace to my heart as I remembered the past with my father and anticipated the future with my stepfather.

Much healing took place in the morning hours.

Eating a leisurely lunch of homemade vegetable soup, made with the tomatoes from my summer garden, nourished my body. Playing the CD player filled my ears and my heart with praise music. Savoring a piece of dark chocolate caused my tongue to tingle with pleasure. Showering in steaming hot water eased the tension in my shoulders.

Eventually, I found my way to the family room hearth. Sitting before the fire relaxed my body. Burning a cinnamon candle permeated the room with a comforting scent. Stacked around me on the floor were boxes of photographs that Mom had given me. I yearned to travel down memory lane, but giving into the cozy warmth, I laid my head down on a pillow instead and dozed off. Waking up slowly, I stretched my arms and legs. Napping restored me, body, mind, and soul. Propping myself up on my elbow, I opened the boxes that held our history. I wanted it to be a delightful jaunt, not a sad one, so sorting through the pictures brought a smile to my lips.

Blinking, the past disappeared. Spotting the clock on the bookcase, I realized that a couple of hours had slipped away while I traveled down the hallways of yesterday.

Wandering back upstairs to the kitchen, I knew supper needed to be started, but something outside of the window caught my eye. A squirrel chased away the birds and was hanging by his tail on the feeder. He entertained me, looking like an acrobat, as he tried to get at the bird seed. After watching him for several minutes, I turned around—both literally and figuratively—with a determination I didn't feel when the day began. With God's help, I was ready to face the future.

Can a broken-down car actually be a blessing? We certainly wouldn't look at it as such. It seemed more of a headache than anything else. But not having a car available forced me to stay home on that particular day, giving me down time that I didn't even know I needed. But God knew. He knew that life was pressing in on me. He knew I needed a bit of pampering. And He used something as unlikely as a broken-down car to accomplish it.

April 2005

The calendar says spring, but the snow flurries outside my window tell me that winter is not yet quite willing to loosen its grip on Northeast Ohio! Longing for warmer weather, my mind wanders back to a morning last summer. For a few months we had been collecting materials to build a patio. I went to bed with the patio on my mind, and when I awoke at 4:30 A.M., the patio was still on my mind! Unable to will myself back to sleep, I slipped out of bed. A cup of blackberry tea and a Philip Keller book kept me busy for about an hour, until my porch beckoned to me. I sat in the rocker, watching and listening to the world wake up. The air was filled with the sounds of birds chirping praises to the Lord. The wind was gently blowing through the tomato plants. The sun was barely visible through the trees. I sat quietly, in awe of God's incredible creation, when the sky suddenly exploded in light as the orange August sun rose above the treetops.

That memory of a summer morning brings warmth to my heart, even while my body is chilled from the frosty temperatures outside. Memories are like that. They have the ability to bring happy thoughts, joy, thankfulness—or at least some memories do. Others can remind us of pain or difficult times in our lives. I wish that I had complete control over these latter kinds of memories, especially the ones that interrupt my sleep in the wee hours of the morning, just before dawn. Yes, there are lessons to be learned from mistakes or trials from the past, but to have them invade my mind in the middle of the night can bring discomfort and anguish. Things always seem to be blown out of proportion when we see them through darkness.

My mom has been tormented over the last few years with memories of her past penetrating her thoughts and haunting her dreams. These come unbidden at all times, but often as she is lying in bed at night when there is nothing to engage her mind. Along with these mental images come regrets or what-ifs. I wonder, is this a normal part of aging? I think perhaps it is for some people as I've experienced it to a smaller degree in my own life. It seems that certain personalities are more prone toward this kind of rumination. Even though I don't have control over the memories and thoughts that barge in, I do have the power of choice over what I allow to linger in my mind. Philippians 4:8–9 says, "Whatever is true, whatever is noble, whatever is right, whatever is pure, whatever is lovely, whatever is admirable—if anything is excellent or praiseworthy—think about such things.... And the God of peace will be with you."

I try to tell Mom that she doesn't have to succumb to the cruel pictures conjured up in her mind. She can receive healing through Christ, along with the peace that passes all worldly understanding. The problem is, she confesses to God repeatedly, but has not been able to receive His forgiveness because she feels unworthy. Nor has she forgiven herself for mistakes that should have been forgotten long ago. The tormentor of our souls must work overtime on elderly hearts and minds. Loneliness. Disappointments. Hopelessness. Sorrows. Sins. Failures.

"If only this, if only that." Praise God that the Redeemer of our souls, He who is within us, is greater than he that is in the world! (see 1 John 4:4b)

I was flipping through an old Bible of mine the other day and came across a statement that I had written in the back, possibly at a time when I was having a hard time forgiving myself: "Christians should erase from their memory the sins God has erased from the record." Good advice. Too often we allow ourselves to be weighed down unnecessarily with burdens that God does not intend for us to carry. They were already carried by our Savior when He was nailed to the cross.

Confessed sin is gone. Let's put it behind us, along with anything else that hinders us from experiencing the grace-filled lives God has always meant for us to have. We need to open our hands and give Him the regrets, the lost dreams, the broken hearts, the abuse, the injustices, or whatever else has afflicted our lives. Easier said than done. My daughter Sarah and I sang a duet once at our church in Chicago. Some of you will recognize this Christian song that was popular in the late '70s. "Give them all, give them all, give them all to Jesus. Shattered dreams, wounded hearts, and broken toys."

Since Mom is having a hard time doing this, I am interceding for her. I want so much for her to have peace in the years she has left on this earth, so I am praying that God would replace her negative memories with positive and pleasant ones and that she would remember the love and the good times. I don't even mind if she would view the past through rose-colored glasses. What harm can it do? Better that than to gaze at yesterday with distorted sight, just as she now sees the physical world around her because of macular degeneration.

The affects of aging on her seem to become more apparent with each passing day—arthritis, osteoporosis, aftermath of a heart attack and open heart surgery. It's really hard to watch her grow old. Dad died when he was 47, so he will forever be young in my mind. But Mom is 78, and it pains me to see what life has done to her, both physically and emotionally. I don't want to remember her as an old woman, but as the vibrant young woman who gave me life, who loved and nurtured me. Some day, in the winter season of my own life, when memories occupy my mind, this is the picture I want to see, the one that I want to remember in my heart:

May 2005

"The Spirit of the Sovereign LORD is on me, because the LORD has anointed me to preach good news to the poor. He has sent me to bind up the brokenhearted, to proclaim freedom for the captives and release from darkness for the prisoners, to proclaim the year of the LORD's favor and the day of vengeance of our God, to comfort all who mourn and provide for those who grieve in Zion—*to bestow on them a crown of beauty instead of ashes, the oil of gladness instead of mourning, and a garment of praise instead of a spirit of despair.* They will be called oaks of righteousness, a planting of the LORD for the display of his splendor" (Isaiah 61:1–3, emphasis mine).

It never fails to amaze me that God can take the darkness of our lives and turn it into something beautiful. He has graciously done it in my life. I've seen Him do it in the lives of others.

As I sat at our computer reading our e-mail one tropical morning, I gasped in shock at the devastating news that traveled through cyberspace from the U.S. to the Philippines. My first instinct was to wrap my arms around my friend, but she was 10,000 miles away. Sending up a prayer, I picked up the telephone receiver, figuring in my head the time difference to Ohio, and then punched in the numbers to make an international call. When I heard her voice on the other end, I lost my composure. My heart was breaking for my friend Mary. Her granddaughter Alyssa died suddenly on September 12, 2002 of a disease that attacks and weakens the heart muscle. I had no words that could take away her incredible pain.

In the two years that we've been back home, I've watched my friend suffer through intense grief. But I've also observed her relationship with the Lord reach new heights. I've seen her passionate to share her pain and her faith with others. Even though Mary and her family are reeling from Alyssa's home-going, they are determined to honor this little girl's memory. God is doing something beautiful through this tragedy. On September 17, 2005, "Alyssa's Hike" will be held at Goodyear Metropolitan Park in Akron where Alyssa frequently hiked with her family. It was organized in order to raise money for two worthy causes— research for Viral Myocarditis (the heart disease that caused Alyssa's death) and a fund dedicated to sending grade school children to Camp Carl (run by The Chapel). Alyssa, like her grandmother, was eager to share her love for Christ with others. She will be smiling down from heaven when she sees those children at camp learn of the God she loves; and her family will know that her death (and short life) was not in vain. *To comfort all who mourn and provide for those who grieve, to bestow on them the oil of gladness instead of mourning.*

The concert I attended recently blessed my heart. As I sat in The Chapel's sanctuary one recent Sunday evening, I marveled at the beautiful woman sharing her heart through song. Julie's beauty is not just of the outward kind. Her inner beauty shines through her eyes and her smile. It's a reflection of her soul, a bruised soul that was healed by the love of Jesus. During the concert, Julie spoke of the depression that afflicted her life, and her husband spoke of the dream that Julie carried in her heart—to write music and to sing songs that would lift up the name of Jesus and encourage the spirits of those who listened. Before the dream could come true, she had to walk the walk. Before she could sing of suffering, she had to know suffering. Before she could share the healing power of Christ, she had to be healed.

God has finally given her the desires of her heart. Julie released a CD last year called "Speak What I Believe." She speaks, or rather sings, with the confidence of one who encountered depression and pain, and who was ultimately rescued by the One she had placed her faith in as a young child. *To bestow on them a garment of praise instead of a spirit of despair.*

I love the way the Lord brings people together. I'm astonished at His timing. Mary and her daughter Sarah (Alyssa's mom) minister through music at The Chapel. Mary plays keyboard, and Sarah was on the worship team with, yes, you guessed it—Julie! Julie had already journeyed through the darkness of pain when Alyssa suddenly died. God had already prepared her to share the healing power of Christ with Mary and Sarah and their family. Julie did this through the way she knows best and what she is gifted in—song. I can't listen to the words that Julie wrote and so beautifully sings without tears running down my cheeks. Here is the song for Alyssa—"Dancing with the Angels"—written, sung, and recorded by Julie Hufstetler:

> She loved to hear the story of the child
> The infant King so tender and so mild
> The baby born that night was the Savior of her life
> Now she'll be spending Christmas 'morn with Him.

It only seems like just the other day
She grabbed her coat and ran outside to play
Now her toys are put away and her bed is always made
And the music of her laugh belongs to heaven.

She'll be dancing with the angels this Christmas
Singing like she's never sung before
Skipping through the streets
Light upon her feet
Dancing with the angels.

She'll celebrate where no one cries a tear
A place that's filled with happiness and cheer
For now her little light shines in Heaven bright
But the heart of me still aches to have her near.

She'll be dancing with the angels this Christmas
Singing like she's never sung before
Skipping through the streets
Light upon her feet
Dancing with the angels.

Merry Christmas, baby
Safe in Jesus' arms
Dancing with the angels.

God transformed Mary's darkness and Julie's darkness into something beautiful. Both women recognize the Lord's miracle of grace in their lives. Both acknowledge His goodness, and both continually give all the glory to Him.

*To bestow on them a crown of beauty instead of ashes. They will be called oaks of righteousness, a planting of the LORD **for the display of His splendor!*** (Emphasis mine.)

June 2005

For the second night in a row, sleep eludes me. Though my eyes are closed, my brain is wide awake. There are circumstances in my life right now that are troubling me. The gentle snoring of my husband lying beside me brings a measure of comfort. I want to snuggle up to him, but I don't want to awaken him. He's been so busy. He needs his sleep.

The first time I glanced at the clock on the bedside table it was 4:20. As I sneak another peek, I silently groan. An hour has passed, and it doesn't seem likely that I will be getting any more sleep. So I roll out of bed, fumble around until my hands find my Bible, and clutching it to my chest, I make my way out to the living room. The sky is just now starting to lighten as a new day begins.

Sitting down on the couch, I open my Bible on my lap, but don't yet start to read. Evidence of my husband's late night studying lies on the coffee table—papers, pens, and his Bible, with its pages open to the book of Ecclesiastes. He's doing a funeral today, and he was preparing his message last night before bed. My eyelids are heavy, and my eyes blurry from the lack of sleep. I'm not sure I'll be able to focus on the words of Scripture lying before me. I close my eyes for a few moments and lay my head on the back of the couch. My thoughts drift to the banquet that Steve and I attended last week at Anthes Restaurant. It was hosted by The Gideons International, a Christian organization that has distributed over one billion copies of God's Word since it was founded in 1899. Many of those Bibles were placed in the hands of people from under-developed areas of the world—people who might never see, much less own, a Bible. That's hard to comprehend as I sit here with a Bible on my lap, one on the coffee table, one in Micah's room, several on the bookcase—hardback, paperback, *King James Version, Living Bible, New American Standard Bible, New*

International Version, English, Tagalog, Greek, Hebrew, Arabic, Latin. How privileged we are!

I'm not sure we fully understand just how fortunate we are to have the Word of God so readily available to us and in our own language! I read a missionary biography recently about a Bible translator in Papua New Guinea. The people she lived among were astounded that God would speak to them in their native tongue and that they could read His words carved into a banana leaf! I've also been reading books on Tyndale and Wycliffe, men who endangered their lives to translate the Bible into English and then get the books into the hands of common men and women. It was against the law for "lower class" people to own or read the Bible. Only those in the upper hierarchy of the church were permitted to read and interpret Scripture.

This reminds me of the church I grew up in. Our lives were not in danger. We were allowed to own a Bible, we were just forbidden to read it! The church has gradually changed its thinking somewhat on this in recent years, for which I am thankful. I just wish God's Word would have been part of my life at an earlier age. I was 25 when He opened my eyes to the truths found in Scripture.

No one should be denied the opportunity, for whatever reason, of reading the Bible or having it read to them. And yet there are still people who have never even heard of the name of Jesus. No one has translated His words and teachings into their language. But praise the Lord, progress is being made. Missionaries are dedicating their lives to this endeavor. Ten distinct languages have been translated into the New Testament and gone to press for several people groups in Peru, Guatemala, Colombia, Bolivia, and Ecuador!

And then there are those countries whose religious leaders will not allow their citizens any access at all to the Bible or Christian material. If they are found with these in their possession, the penalty could be death. "Is this the day?" Li Quan awoke to these words every day of his adult life. Li Quan is a character in the book *Safely Home* by Randy Alcorn that I read last summer. The novel is about the persecuted church in China. It had a tremendous impact on me as I contemplated what believers in Christ around the world face each and every day. Possibly the first thoughts they wake up with in the morning, just as Li Quan, are: "Is this the day that I will be persecuted, be tortured, be martyred, die for my faith?" Even though they face this danger, the Scriptures are so precious to them that they will risk everything to have the very words of God clasped in their hands or hidden in their hearts. Do I treasure my Bible in the same way?

There was an article in the religion section of our local newspaper: "Holy Book not to Be Worshiped" by Steve Gushee. This came out of the current alleged reports of U.S. military personnel desecrating a Quran by flushing it down a toilet. Mr. Gushee wrote, "Holy books are critical to the preservation and growth of a religious tradition, but they are not divine. They are not gods and are not to be worshiped. They are simply books made holy by association with the divine, not by inherent divinity. The tendency to make idols of the words of religious teachers is endemic among what is tellingly called the religions of the Book: Judaism, Christianity, and Islam." I found his statements interesting, especially coming out of a so-called "Christian" culture in the Philippines where an object (i.e. Bible) could be made into an idol and viewed as something that has a special power. There *is* power, but the power is not the Book itself. I can't touch the Book and be healed. Rather, it's when the words of the Book touch my heart, when I allow the very heart of God, as revealed through these words, to change my life. I don't make a god out of the Bible and worship it. I worship the God of the Bible.

Unlike the Quran and any other religious book, there is power in the words of the Bible, because they are words of life from a living God. "For the word of God is living and active and sharper than any two-edged sword, and piercing as far as the division of soul and spirit, of both joints and marrow, and able to judge the thoughts and intentions of the heart" (Hebrews 4:12 *NASB*).

I open my eyes and focus them on the words in the book that is sitting on my lap. How awesome that God would speak to me in my native tongue! Because of the sacrifices that men and women have made throughout history, I can sit here any time I want and read my Bible. May I never get so complacent that I take for granted the cost that they paid. And may I always treasure this book, for it is the source of my strength, comfort, forgiveness, healing, and joy. It's the place I go when I'm troubled or worried. It's where I find acceptance and peace. In its pages I discover the One who loves me with an everlasting love. How could I not treasure it?!

July 2005 #1

I boarded the airplane not knowing if I would see my step-father alive again. Earlier that morning, my doctor gave me the results of my medical tests that had the potential to have serious consequences for me, but thankfully, turned out to be something manageable. Add into the equation the reason I was in the airplane. I was flying to Virginia to be with my daughter Sarah and my son-in-law Brandon, who would soon be parents. Sarah would be giving birth to their first child by c-section the next day. It's no wonder my blood pressure was abnormally high!

Shortly after takeoff, I looked out the window. We were floating above the clouds, with the earth visible through the gaps. As always, God's majesty took my breath away! My heart sang out: "Be exalted, O God, above the heavens. Let Thy glory be over all the earth." I then settled back in my seat for the short trip and opened Sheila Walsh's book *Extraordinary Faith*.

As we started the descent into Reagan National Airport, I again looked out the window. The scene was spectacular, even though it was man-made! Washington D.C. lay before my eyes—the Lincoln Memorial, the Capitol Building, and other significant buildings in this amazing city. It was rather an astonishing experience to see my country's capital from the sky!

I called home on my cell phone as I waited outside the airport. The news I received was not what I was expecting. My stepfather had had a pacemaker put in while I was up in the air. This meant that the Lord was graciously giving him some extra time.

Sarah and Brandon picked me up, and we spent a leisurely evening, eating out at a Mexican restaurant and then watching a bit of television in their apartment. The next morning we made our way to the hospital. There was a lot of activity going on in the maternity ward! As we sat down to wait, I took advantage of the time and prayed with Sarah and Brandon. Before long, they took Sarah back to be prepped, and I found myself alone in the fathers' waiting room. Just as I felt some anxiety in the pit of my stomach, Brandon's parents walked in. They had driven down from Ohio that morning. I can't really say that I waited patiently. I intermittently talked with Cheryl and paced the hallway. Finally, Brandon walked in. I literally jumped out of the chair! He accompanied us grandparents to the nursery and pointed out our new granddaughter! We all thought for sure it was a boy! As I gazed at that sweet little face, I fell instantly in love! I remember thinking: *How much love can a heart hold?* I wanted to stand at the window and stare at her forever, but my motherly concern for Sarah was strong, so Brandon took us to the recovery room. She was anxiously waiting for us so she could reveal the baby's name. Elena Grace!

Light and grace. I pray that as she grows she will be a shining light for Jesus, extending His grace in this dark world.

After the excitement had tapered off a bit, I leaned down to whisper in Sarah's ear. With tears in my eyes, I said, "You didn't know this, but my dad, your grandfather, died on this day in 1968." Tears glistened in her eyes as I then told her, "Now I have a happy memory of this day."

Over the next few days, Brandon and I took turns staying all night at the hospital with Sarah and Elena. On the day they were released, I was at their apartment to welcome them home. Since my time in Virginia was limited, I had every intention of making the most of it. I was there to help. I changed the sheets on the bed, did laundry, took the trash out, and packed several boxes in preparation for their upcoming move to a larger apartment. But most importantly, I bonded with my granddaughter. I didn't even mind that I lost sleep rocking Elena in the early morning hours while her mommy got some rest. Occasionally, Sarah would catch me staring at her. I was storing up the picture of my daughter tenderly cradling her daughter in her arms—an image to treasure in my heart when the miles separated us. Sarah wasn't the only one I enjoyed watching, though. What fun I had observing my son-in-law interact with his daughter. Oh my! Elena already had him wrapped around her little finger! She certainly captured her daddy's heart!

The days flew by much too quickly. Before I knew it, I was on my way back to the airport. Once again, as has happened so many times in the past when I said goodbye to loved ones, my heart was torn in two. How I yearn for the day "goodbye" will no longer be part of my vocabulary. As the plane took off, I stared out the window, and with tears blurring my vision, I watched Washington D.C. disappear from view. The closer I got to Ohio, the further away Virginia seemed to be. I knew that I was not going to like long-distance grandparenting. As the years go by, I am realizing more and more what my mother went through during our time in the Philippines. She often felt deprived of her grandchildren 10,000 miles away. 10,000 miles away? Suddenly Virginia didn't seem quite so far away after all. And yet it's not close enough, because there's a little girl there who has firmly staked her claim on my heart.

July 2005 #2

It's a surreal experience to watch someone die. We sat staring at his chest go up and down, up and down with each breath, waiting for the moment that his chest would not rise again. Even when that moment came, we continued to watch, refusing to believe that he was really gone.

My stepfather Paul departed this life on Monday, June 27, my husband's birthday. He left much sooner than we expected. The pacemaker had been put in 20 days earlier. He seemed to be doing well, and we anticipated that he would be with us for months rather than days.

Mom and I spent several hours with him in the emergency room the previous Friday. He had been complaining of headaches after a nasty fall a few weeks earlier. CT scan showed that there was no bleeding, no skull fracture, no trace of cancer in his brain. As we waited for the results of a chest x-ray, I kept wondering if I should talk to him again about eternal issues. But I sat there, thinking that I had plenty of time. When I noticed that his eyes were a bit glassy and he was pointing at something I couldn't see, I felt an urgency that this was indeed the time to speak. I'm sure it was the Lord who prompted me to get up out of my chair, walk over to the bed, and take Paul's hand. I asked him if he was okay. His eyes focused on me, and I knew he was listening. He said, "Yes. Why?" I told him I was worried about him and wanted to make sure that he was ready. He said he was. I said, "I want to make sure your heart is ready." He thought I was referring to his physical heart, so I rephrased it and asked if his soul was ready. He kept saying he believed in his Maker. I told him he had to do more than believe in his Maker, he had to believe in the Savior. He answered with, "I believe in the good Lord." I continued the discussion, reiterating that Jesus died for our sins and that we needed to confess to Him in order to be saved, that He was the only way to heaven—we can't trust in our own good works. Throughout the conversation, I was convinced that he was lucid. My hope, even now, is that he fully understood the ramifications of not trusting in the finished work of Christ.

The chest x-ray revealed congestive heart failure. The doctor released him from the ER with instructions to increase his medication. I drove Mom and Paul to their house, went to the pharmacy to pick up refills, and then went home. The next day my mother called to tell me that she'd had a rough night with Paul. He was saying crazy things, and she'd had a hard time calming him down. I went back over, and we waited together for the hospice nurse to come. When she arrived, she assessed the situation. It was her opinion that the process of dying had begun. We were shocked. My daughter Ruthanne and my aunt came over. One minute he recognized them and the next he was confused. He started getting agitated, and we had a difficult time keeping him in his recliner. The nurse gave him some medication to calm him down. She was a blessing, sitting with us for several hours and making sure that Paul was comfortable. Eventually everyone left, but I knew that I couldn't leave my mom alone for the night. She slept on the couch next to his recliner, and I slept upstairs. Thankfully, Paul slept through the night. But when we tried to awaken him in the morning to give him his medication, we couldn't arouse him. We figured that what the nurse gave him was helping him sleep. I called hospice, and the nurse I spoke with told me to let him sleep, to not worry about his medication. I decided to go home, shower, and attend the Sunday worship service.

Ruthanne went back over to the house after church. Paul's son, who is a doctor in Boston, called before I returned. He spoke to Ruthanne, who is a nurse, and asked her to check Paul's pupils. When she told him what she observed, he confirmed that his father was in a coma. And so the vigil began. Again, just like the evening before, Mom and I were eventually alone in the house. About 11:00 I went upstairs to try to get some sleep. I lay there in bed listening for any noise that might mean the end was near.

Since death seemed so close, my mind was filled with thoughts of dying. I sat up, turned on the light, and called home to talk to Steve. I asked him, "I think the angels come for someone who believes in Christ, but what happens when an unbeliever dies?" He said we don't really know. I have to admit that there was some fear in my heart, because I honestly could not say one way or another where Paul stood with Christ. I kept thinking that at the moment he died I would hear an evil laugh and a voice would say, "He's mine, he's mine!" Steve prayed for me and asked the Lord to calm my anxious heart and my overactive imagination. I needed God's presence and comfort, so I read through several Psalms before I turned out the light. I spent a fitful night, waking up every 15 minutes or so. Every time I opened my eyes, I pleaded with the Lord to have mercy on Paul. I felt like I was in a battle for his soul.

About 4:00 Mom called my name. I ran downstairs. The gurgling sound had started from Paul's throat. I ran back upstairs to retrieve my Bible. Sitting down next to his chair, I read aloud Psalm 23. Mom and I both then stood next to him with our hands on his shoulders, reassuring him that we loved him and it was alright to go. I placed a chair next to his recliner so Mom could sit down, and I sat on the couch. Suddenly, his eyes opened. He stared straight ahead, then moved his eyes to the side where my mom sat, and looked at her. It probably was not more than ten seconds, but I believe it was a gift from God, that it was Paul's way of saying goodbye. He closed his eyes, took several more labored breaths, and then was gone. There was no evil laughter or voice. Paul died peacefully, just the way he wanted to. No pain—in his recliner—at home.

We buried his ashes two days later next to his first wife and his son. The service consisted of the Veterans of Foreign Wars' 12-gun salute, and a representative presented my mother with the American flag. A Catholic lay woman read prayers, his oldest son spoke of his father and read two poems, his daughter-in-law read a prayer, and Steve finished up with a clear presentation of the good news of Jesus Christ. As we sat there at the cemetery in the heat of the day, I looked around at my family in attendance. My daughter Sarah, son-in-law Brandon, and new granddaughter Elena had driven up from Virginia for the funeral. Little Elena was just three weeks old. My daughter Ruthanne, heavy with child, sat under the shade of a tree as my son-in-law Ryan stood off to the side with my granddaughter Audrey. My son Micah, a junior in college, looked tall and hand-some as he stood close by. My daughter Hester was in Europe (Macedonia) leading a short-term mission team. We discussed before she left what she should do if something happened to her grandfather. She was to stay and finish what the Lord had given her to do. We never really expected that his death would occur this early. I e-mailed her with the news—I'm thankful for modern modes of communication. She was able to make an international call to talk with her grandmother the day before the funeral. We knew that even though she couldn't be there physically, she was present in spirit.

As I write this, several days have passed since Paul's death. My mood has been pensive. Life can seem so puzzling to me at times. In a matter of weeks, a baby was born—a man died—a woman was widowed for a second time—another baby is expected soon. A new generation comes into existence as an old generation gradually fades away. The cycle of life completes itself while another cycle begins. Good things happen. Bad things happen. Joy. Suffering. If it weren't for my faith in Christ and my hope for eternity with Him, it would all seem futile. If I weren't convinced that God is sovereign and in control, I would struggle to find meaning in it all. Sheila Walsh, in her book *Extraordinary Faith*, writes, "Faith requires great trust and rock-solid belief in the promises of God. Following Christ is a direct call to let go of our human need to understand everything and trust God." It's as simple as that. Even though life doesn't seem to make sense at times, and even though I don't always understand what God is doing, I need to rest in His sovereign timing and perfect plan, to have absolute trust in His faithfulness and goodness. So when the difficult is mixed in with the wonderful, I can still claim the promise: "The Lord is my Shepherd, I shall not want. He makes me lie down in green pastures; He leads me beside quiet waters…Even though I walk through the valley of the shadow of death, I will fear no evil, for You are with me" (Psalm 23).

July 2005 #3

A slide show flashed across my mind. I saw: a sweet baby cuddled in my arms—a tiny tot with blond curls and an impish grin sitting inside our kitchen cabinet in our Chicago apartment—an ornery little tyke hiding her slippers from her daddy in the broiler of the stove—a cute toddler lying in bed between Sarah and Ruthanne—a small child sitting sound asleep on her grandpa's lap on a lounge chair in his backyard—a persistent little girl lining up her stuffed animals on her bed in South Carolina—a five year old with her arm in a cast, standing between her buddies, twins Jon and Josh, when we lived across the street from The Chapel—a kindergartener wearing her red and green plaid uniform attending Chapel Hill

Christian School—a first grader sitting at the table in our house in a provincial town of the Philippines doing her home school assignments—the only blond in a sea of dark hair riding in a bicycle sidecar with her Filipino friends—an elementary school student marching around the campus of Faith Academy for Filipinana week—a middle school student at outdoor education week wearing a hat she made—an eighth grader trying to figure out who she was—a ninth grader playing her flute at a recital—a soccer player at CVCA and Faith Academy—an FA high school graduate standing on stage as they announced that she was valedictorian of her class—a beautiful bridesmaid at her sisters' weddings—a college student with Rachel, her best friend from Faith Academy—a world traveler standing with me on the cliffs of Ireland, looking out over the Irish Sea—a young woman in cap and gown at Messiah College graduation—a graduate student with her Korean friends, studying linguistics in the Philippines—a big sister with her little brother Micah at his high school graduation—a proud aunt holding her niece Audrey. The years seemed to fly quickly by as the pictures flashed across my memory. I had the strange compulsion to put my mind on "pause," to stop the years from progressing any further. I guess it's possible to do that for a short while, but then we realize that time goes on. Besides, our children don't want to be stuck in the past—they have a future to live.

The event that has sparked my nostalgic pictorial journey is Hester's engagement. Yes, my little girl is getting married! Dale Dailey proposed to her on Monday, July 11th—his birthday. I asked him if it was his birthday present to himself, and he answered with a resounding "YES!" As parents, Steve and I are extremely pleased. I made the statement to Dale that he is an answer to our prayers. And he is! So much so that when I learned of their engagement, I cried tears of joy in my husband's arms as I thanked the Lord for His working in our daughter's life.

The transition for our children back and forth from an Asian culture to an American one has not always been easy. In a letter that Hester sent out as she was preparing to lead a short-term mission team to Macedonia this summer she wrote, "As many of you may know, the past few years have been a time of extreme transition for me. After graduating from college, God gave me the wonderful opportunity to study and teach in the Philippines for a year before He called me back to Ohio. The shift from Asia back to the U.S. has been a challenging one for me, but even in this tumultuous time, God has shown His faithfulness. He has been patient with me and has showered me with grace; He has blessed me far beyond anything I could have imagined."

God indeed has blessed Hester by bringing Dale into her life. (And might I add that God has blessed Dale by bringing Hester into his life!) At the right time, and in the right place (The Chapel), He brought them together. And in April we will welcome this wonderful young man into our family.

The next nine months will be filled with activity as we make plans for the wedding. In the midst of the busyness, I know there are bound to be moments of both joy and sadness for me. It just happens to be the way I'm wired. I'm ever so grateful for a husband who helps me to stay grounded and to view life with a different perspective. Steve won't be insensitive and brush aside my motherly emotions; however, I'm sure he will encourage me to make every effort to enter into the excitement and anticipation of what the future holds for Hester and Dale rather than trying to hold on to "my little girl," because she's not my little girl any longer. She has transformed into the beautiful young woman God created her to be and will one day soon be the wife of the man she loves. And yet...and yet, hidden away in the secret places of my heart, Hester will always be that cute little toddler with the blond curls and an impish grin.

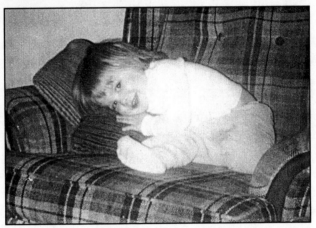

August 2005 #1

Just how much love is a human heart capable of holding? As I cradled my granddaughter Elena in my arms last month, gazing down at her sweet little face, my heart felt so full that I wasn't sure I could squeeze any more love into it. But I was wrong. My newest granddaughter has proven that a grandmother's heart can expand to accommodate however many grandchildren the Lord blesses her life with. Maddie, from the moment I laid my eyes on her, filled a part of my heart reserved just for her.

Ruthanne gave birth to Ryan's and her second daughter and our third grandchild on July 15. My daughter gave me permission to be present for the birth. The plan for me to be with Sarah when she gave birth in June did not happen because of the scheduled c-section. Only Brandon could be in the room. When Ruthanne gave birth to Audrey in October, 2003, she just wanted Ryan with her. I totally understood. I'm not sure why the change in heart this time, but I'm grateful. This incredible experience allowed me to encounter both ends of the life spectrum just 18 days apart. I was a spectator of death and of birth—my stepfather departing this world and my granddaughter entering this world.

It's beyond my comprehension how anyone could witness a birth and still refuse to believe in the Creator. A miracle unfolded right before my eyes! It was amazing! The only difficult part for me was watching my daughter endure the pain. They call it labor for a reason! She worked hard to deliver that baby. I wanted to help her, but no one could do the work for her. All I was able to do was brush Ruthanne's hair from her forehead and *pray*. I well remembered the urge to get my own babies out! One last push, and Madelyn Rose literally popped out, drew her first breath, and let out a wail. I was not only filled with awe at this miracle, but also with praise to my God who created this little one so perfectly. Tears ran down my cheeks, even while I wore a silly grin on my face. I just couldn't stop smiling *or* crying! Through my blurred vision, I noticed that Ryan was also overcome with emotion. I love to see these tender sides of my sons-in-law that I don't normally see.

Madelyn Rose! Madelyn means "high tower." As her name indicates, I pray that she will grow up to be a woman of strength, offering Christ's fragrance of life to a dying world.

Shortly after her birth, Madelyn was wrapped in a blanket and laid on her mommy's breast. There's something so enchanting about the look on a mother's face as she lovingly gazes into the face of her child. I see it on Sarah's face; I see it on Ruthanne's face. Can there be anything more beautiful than that picture? I imagine Mary had the same look when she gazed at her newborn son, Jesus. It's a universal phenomenon. Women around the world and throughout the ages have experienced the magic, the wonder of bringing forth new life. What a gift from the Lord! What a blessing to be a woman! What a joy to be a mother! What a delight to be a grandmother!

August 2005 #2

28, 81, 65, 1
That's not a quarterback calling the play. Those are the statistics that tell me that death is not a respecter of persons. Young man. Old man. Middle-aged woman. Small child. It makes no difference.

He's the son of missionaries in Africa. His parents received the call that all parents dread—their son was killed in a car accident.
He died on April 26, 2005. He was *28* years old.

He's my stepfather. He was married to my mother for 29 years. He was diagnosed with cancer of the esophagus in March.
He died on June 27, 2005. He was *81* years old.

She's my cousin. She was diagnosed with ovarian cancer eight years ago. Her husband was killed in a car accident in 2001. She fought a good fight, but lost the battle.
She died on July 1, 2005. She was *65* years old.

He's the son of friends (a pastor and his wife). He was diagnosed with spina bifida before birth. He underwent surgery for a malignant brain tumor before his first birthday.
He died on July 25, 2005. He was *one* year old.

When a person dies at 81, there is sadness that he is no longer with us, but we somehow rationalize that he lived a long life. When a person dies at 65, there is sorrow that her life was finished too soon. When a person dies at 28, there is shock because he was in the prime of life. When a person dies at one, we stop understanding. Grief is real no matter what the age. But when a small child dies, our finite minds just cannot grasp how this can be, or why this seemingly senseless thing has happened.

My husband Steve and I had planned to fly to Philadelphia on Tuesday to spend a couple of days with friends. Instead, we took an emergency flight on Monday evening, arriving at the hospital at midnight. We didn't get there in time—their baby had died at 6:30 P.M. His parents were already sequestered in a room, grieving the death of their son. We sat in the waiting room outside the Connelly Center for Families at Children's Hospital of Philadelphia, feeling a bit like sentinels, guarding them from the outside world. Prayer was our weapon. Finally, at 3:00 A.M., we decided to get some sleep. I stretched out on a couch, and Steve lay on the floor with a chair cushion for a pillow. We awoke at 5:50 A.M, and our friend emerged from the room about 20 minutes later. What can you possibly say at a time like this? Not much of anything. We both hugged him and assured him that we were there to help in any way they wanted. Steve assisted him in packing up the baby's hospital room, while I sat in the waiting room, continuing to "guard" the baby's mother. At 9:00 A.M, as instructed by the father, I walked down the hallway to the room where the mother was sleeping. The raw pain I saw on her face when I opened the door to wake her up took the breath right out of me. It felt like someone had punched me in the stomach. My mother's heart was breaking for this young woman.

Throughout the day, Steve and I ran errands and did whatever they needed us to do. I hope that merely our presence was a measure of comfort to them. That evening the four of us gathered to pray. Before we approached the Throne of Grace, our friends wanted to talk. We listened. They wept. We wept. Occasionally we tried to offer words that might console. I can only hope that I didn't say something stupid or insensitive. My friend Mary says, "We ask God to keep the words that are helpful and throw out the rest." Please, Lord.

There were intervals of silence as we let them think through what they were feeling. When my friend whispered of holding her baby in her arms as he took his last breath, I remembered how I felt recently watching my daughters cradling their babies in their arms. These two pictures of mothers tenderly holding their children were similar—the love was the same, but the circumstances were not. I just could not reconcile the differences in my mind, couldn't accept the anguish in one, the joy in the other. We spent much time in heart-wrenching, tearful prayer.

They flew home early the next morning. They were anxious to return to their two children. How do you tell a five-year-old and a three-year-old that their baby brother is not coming home? We prayed throughout the day for grace and wisdom.

Calling hours for the baby were at The Chapel on Thursday, July 28th—my birthday. Both Steve's birthday and my birthday have been shadowed by death this summer. We just didn't feel much like celebrating. We did join hundreds of people, though, on Friday to celebrate the baby's life. This little boy, though he was only among us for 14 months, probably touched more lives than many adults have in a lifetime. As the video played on the screen in the front of the sanctuary, we couldn't help but smile, because the pictures of him were lighting up the room with his beautiful eyes and endearing smile. You could tell he felt loved. There has been so much love and courage portrayed in this precious family.

We continue to grieve with them, but not without hope, for we know that the baby is safe in the arms of Jesus, and some day there will be a wonderful reunion in heaven, However, as hard as it is to understand, life here goes on. That promised reunion seems so far away. But in the reality of eternity, it's just a moment in time. There's so much to look forward to. When we finally step through that curtain into heaven, with Jesus by our side, this little one will be waiting there on the other side to thank us for praying for him and to welcome us home. Home where there will be no more pain, no more tears, no more goodbyes. Forever.

> *And when we stand before the One with nail prints in*
> *His hands*
> *The memories of pain will be so far*
> *And all that will remain are His scars. (Julie Hufstetler)*

September 2005

The summer storms were intense. The booming thunder and flashing lightning woke us up in the middle of the night. The thunder was so loud that I jumped every time it rumbled. At last there was calm, and we drifted off to sleep, only to be awakened again by a second storm. More of the same. Then calm once again, until a third storm rolled in. The whole night seemed electrically charged as the lightning lit up our bedroom.

Electrically charged—that kind of describes my whole summer. Or maybe emotionally charged would be more appropriate. Times of elation. Times of sorrow. Highs and lows—like a roller coaster. I remember standing in line at Cedar Point Amusement Park when I was younger, waiting to get on the gigantic roller coaster, trembling with both fear and excitement. Then, sitting in the car, strapped in, anticipating the exhilaration of climbing those hills and then plunging down into the valleys. Up, down. Up again, down again. I can still feel the funny sensation in the pit of my stomach.

I'm anxious to get off my emotional roller coaster and walk on level ground for awhile. My head is spinning with all that's happened this summer. I'm eager for a bit of calm. Lord willing, autumn will bring me some sense of restfulness and tranquility.

The start of school is a sure indication that autumn is near. My husband Steve and I drove our son Micah back to Wheaton College on August 21. The drive through Ohio and Indiana was beautiful. The trees already were tinged with color. I savored the pastoral scenery as we listened to a praise CD. The choruses were the same ones that we sang with our Filipino brothers and sisters. Hearing the familiar music triggered memories. We almost could have been traveling in the Philippines! Instead of cows grazing, though, we would have seen carabao grazing. Instead of acres of cornfields, we would have seen acres of rice fields. Instead of driving from Ohio to Illinois, we would have been driving from Manila to Bulacan.

I had a momentary childhood flashback when we drove through South Bend, Indiana. My head automatically turned to the left, searching for the golden dome of the University of Notre Dame. Sure enough, there it was, bringing back memories of my dad. We visited the college one summer when I was about six years old. Dad was a huge fan of the Fighting Irish football team! Whenever he watched a game on our television set at home, he made me stand up and sing the Victory March. I still know the words to this day! "Cheer, cheer for old Notre Dame, wake up the echoes cheering her name ..."

When we got close to the Illinois border, Steve was ready for me to take the wheel. He had been driving since we left the house at 5:30 in the morning. As I slid into the driver's seat, I popped in a different CD—Julie Hufstetler's *Speak What I Believe*. We enjoyed listening to the wonderful music and thought-provoking lyrics, but I probably should have turned it off before the last song started. I always cry when Julie sings "Dancing with the Angels." It was not a good time for me to be driving in the heavy traffic on the outskirts of Chicago, my eyes blurred with tears!

As we drove by Cicero Avenue, my thoughts naturally turned to the three years we lived in the Chicago suburb of Cicero while Steve attended Moody Bible Institute. Those were particularly lean years for us as we struggled to make ends meet, at times finding it difficult to feed our family of five. But God always faithfully, and miraculously, provided for our needs. Oh, the stories I could tell! Even back then, before we knew we were headed for the mission field, He was preparing us.

Early afternoon we pulled into the parking lot of Wheaton College. After Steve helped Micah unload the car and carry suitcases and boxes up to his new dorm room, we had a tailgate picnic. That sparked another memory. One day, while living in Chicago, we yearned to get out of the "concrete" city. We drove up to Wheaton and had a picnic on the college campus. It was lovely to be able to sit on the green grass under the shade of a tree, to be able to see the blue sky and hear the birds twittering. Our three daughters had fun running around the open space. Micah was not even a twinkle in our eyes on that day 25 years ago, and here he was, getting ready to start his junior year at that same college we had visited long before he was born.

Leaving him to get his room set up, we went to check into our hotel. Later, we took him out for supper. Before I knew it, it was time to say goodbye. There's that nasty word again. Will I ever get used to it? No, I don't think so. I tearfully hugged him, holding on and not wanting to let go, wishing he was a little boy again. It was such a joy to have him home for the summer that I know I'll miss having him around.

Well, Julie seems to have the knack for making me cry. "There Goes My Heart" was playing on the CD player as we drove off campus. She wrote this song with her three sons in mind. "There goes my heart again, walking around outside of me. Getting on the school bus, leaving for the day. Heading off to somewhere I won't be." By that time, I was almost sobbing! And then she sang: "So many days You've brought us through, You'll take us through the rest. My heart can safely trust in You, even when it's beating out my chest." There it is—the bottom line—trust. Safely trust. Entrusting my son into God's safe, capable, and loving hands. "And I pray, I pray God bless their day. Guide them in Your special way. Give them courage, Lord, to do what's right. Bring them safely home to me tonight. There goes my heart." Thanks, Julie, for singing the prayer of your mother's heart—the one that all mothers can relate to, especially this one!

God, please bless my son. Guide him in Your special way. Give him courage, Lord, to do what's right. Bring Micah safely home to me at Thanksgiving. There goes my heart.

Micah—second grade

October 2005

While browsing around the Hartville Marketplace recently, I happened on a small shop called "My Daughters and Me." The name itself was enough to draw me inside, but the clincher was the sign saying the shop was closing and everything was 30 percent off! I wandered in. A wooden plaque caught my eye. These words were painted on it: *FINALLY HOME this is where I belong.* I could envision just the right spot in my bedroom where I could hang it—a place where I would see it every morning when I woke up. As I stood at the counter paying for it, the owner asked if it was a gift for someone or if it was for me. I told her it was for me, that we had lived overseas for several years and we were *Finally Home!* She told me about another woman who bought the same plaque. Her husband had been in the military, stationed in Iraq, and he was *Finally Home.*

Home. It means something different to everyone. Often when we were *home* in Akron from the Philippines on furlough, people would comment: "I bet you're ready to go back *home.*" I always found it difficult to respond to that statement, not wanting to disillusion them about my missionary commitment. I wanted to say, "I'm already *home!*" I know that there are many missionary women around the world who consider their host countries to be their *home.* I never felt that way. The Philippines was never *home* for me. Sometimes I experienced guilt over those feelings, but I couldn't hide the truth—my heart was always right here in Northeast Ohio. That doesn't mean that I didn't leave pieces of my heart in the Philippines, because I did—I left a part of me with each of my precious friends. But the essence of who I am is here in this part of the world, where my history is. It's the place *where I belong.*

Home for me growing up was a small, two-bedroom apartment. I was an only child, extremely shy and lonely. My mother, at times, was overprotective. My father, at times, found it difficult to show affection. I, at times, lived in a dream world. My focus in this imaginary world was always a house. My childish mind believed that this was the key to happiness, because if I lived in a house I would have brothers and sisters and there would be lots of laughter and fun and I wouldn't be shy or lonely anymore. Looking back, I now recognize that I was searching for love and acceptance and security. For some reason I tied that into living in a house, probably because of observing the families of school friends who lived in houses rather than apartments. As I entered my high school years, the daydreams took a bit of a different twist. Instead of a house filled with brothers and sisters, my mythical house was occupied by a husband and several children.

It seemed that my dreams were on the way to being fulfilled when Steve and I married in 1972. I gave birth to our first child in 1973. And in 1974 we bought our first house. But even though this was what I had longed for and even though there was a measure of happiness in our lives, Steve and I both realized that something was missing. We didn't have a clue what it was, and we often pursued it in superficial things or in the wrong places—until the summer of 1976 when our lives were changed by the power of the Holy Spirit. That's when Jesus Christ graciously saved us!

We started attending The Chapel where God began to fill the void and help us to grow spiritually while strengthening our marriage. Finally, we really did have it all. We would live in our house in Ellet for the rest of our lives, raising our children there. Or so I thought. The Lord had something totally different in mind. God led Steve to answer a call at The Chapel for full-time pastoral ministry. He applied and was accepted at Moody Bible Institute and eventually was laid off from his job at Firestone Tire and Rubber Company. We sold our house and headed for Chicago in 1979 with two children and another on the way. This was only the beginning of a journey that has included 21 different houses and apartments.

Midway through our three years in Chicago, the Lord changed our direction. Actually, He didn't change it, since He had it planned all along—He just didn't tell us about it right away! We began praying about missions. After graduation, we packed up our three children and moved to Columbia, South Carolina so Steve could attend graduate school. A year-and-a-half later, we were back at The Chapel where Steve did a missions internship. And then in 1986, we traveled to the other side of the world with four children and began a ministry in the Philippines which stretched over the next 17 years.

Even though I had a personal relationship with Christ, a loving husband, four great kids (three daughters and a son), and was serving the Lord—everything I needed to bring joy and fulfillment—there remained a sense of discontent, because still tucked away in a corner of my heart was that childhood desire to have a house of my own. Not just anywhere in the world, mind you—it had to be *home*—in or near Akron, Ohio.

In every place we lived throughout the years of our married life, I endeavored to make a comfortable *home* for my family, but the longing of that lonely little girl lingered. Each time we came back to the States from the Philippines on furlough, I hoped and prayed that this would be the time I would see my dream realized, only for the Lord to say "Not yet. The time isn't right. Wait." And He would send us back for another term. Each time we returned to the field, I asked Him to take away the yearning for a real *home* and for roots. Either He chose not to, or I chose not to completely give up my dream. I wondered if the time would ever be right, if I'd ever see my desire fulfilled on this side of eternity.

As we launched into our fourth term of service, after a struggle deep in my heart, I finally yielded, opening my hands and giving the Lord my desire for a house. If I never lived in a house that truly belonged to me, it was okay. I would continue to faithfully serve Him. Once I unclenched my tightly closed fists, relinquishing my dream to Him, something started to happen. Not only did God work in my heart during that time, but also the seeds for our future that He had planted in my husband's heart, the ones that had sent down roots over the years, were starting to germinate. Our son would graduate from high school at the end of this four-year term, our two married daughters talked of wanting to start families, and our parents were getting older. Steve was sensing that it was time to finish up our overseas missionary career. He was feeling a need and desire to be with family. And so we began to pray once again for our future. Some of our closest prayer partners prayed with us, asking God to place us where He could use our experiences as missionaries as well as our spiritual gifts. These friends were very specific in their prayers, asking Him to allow us to minister at The Chapel. This had been part of our vision from the beginning—had always been our hope. The timing couldn't have been more perfect as the new campus in Green, a suburb south of downtown Akron, was scheduled to be finished at the end of our term. Correspondence flew across the ocean via e-mail between Steve and three of our pastors. I can still remember the stressful waiting and then the tears of joy and relief when Steve opened the e-mail that held an invitation to join The Chapel staff. We were going *home*!

As I communicated by e-mail with friends who knew that I collected "hearts," I sort of jokingly typed: "Wouldn't it be wonderful if I could live in HEART-ville?!" My prayer circle took it seriously and got on their knees. These seven terrific women boldly asked the Lord to give me a house in Hartville. My dream resurfaced. I wasn't even aware that it was still tucked away in the recesses of my heart. Could it have been that God was the One who had placed it there? After all, He created me as a woman—with maternal and "nesting" instincts. So I started to pray along with my friends. But doubts would barge in, and questions would find their way into my mind: *How can we afford a house? How can I selfishly ask for a house when I'm surrounded by such poverty in this third world country? I don't deserve a house, why would God want to give me a house?* Sharon, one of my prayer circle friends, lovingly rebuked me, reminding me that none of us deserves anything, but God delights in giving us good gifts.

Micah graduated from Faith Academy on May 28, and on May 29, we were *finally home.* June first found us sitting in the new sanctuary at the new Green campus, thanking the Lord not only for how He had provided for and blessed The Chapel with this wonderful new facility, but also that we could be part of it all.

Then, exactly three months after we stepped back on to U.S. soil, on August 29, 2003, my dream finally became a reality when two retired missionary women handed over the keys to our new *home* in HARTVILLE! The story of how this happened has God's handprint all over it.

Each and every day I marvel at how the Lord not only gifted us with this *home*, but also that He delighted in giving me a house in Hartville! I imagine Him looking down at me and smiling with such tenderness and saying, "I never forgot the yearnings of that little girl who longed for a house full of love. I asked you to wait because I had many things to show you and teach you. You had to learn to trust Me and to know that I alone am the source of your love and security. And now that the time is right, the wait is over, and I am pleased to give you this house—simply because I love you."

November 2005

The country road was deserted. Pumpkins were scattered in a farm field to my right. A roadside stand held colorful mums for sale. It was kind of a gloomy day, with rain falling and dark clouds overhead. As I approached the crest of a small hill, a red barn caught my eye. That's when I saw it—a rainbow arcing in the sky above the barn, with the sun peeking through the clouds. I closed my eyes briefly and whispered, "Thank You, Jesus." Then burst into tears.

The rainbow has always been a symbol of hope. Thousands of years have passed since God first used the rainbow as a sign of His covenant to Noah in Old Testament times. And here it is, the year 2005, and God is still placing His rainbow in the sky to assure us that He does not forget His promises.

On that particular gloomy day that I was driving down that country road, I was headed toward the hospital. My mother was in the coronary care unit with pneumonia. This came on her rather suddenly.

Monday morning I took her shopping, and then we had lunch. She had a doctor's appointment in the afternoon for a regular checkup. Everything looked good. But then she called me on Tuesday and said she wasn't feeling well. We figured it was some sort of a flu bug. She planned to take it easy and have some chicken noodle soup for lunch.

It's amazing how fast you can wake up from a deep sleep at the sound of the telephone ringing. Your heart seems to stop as the shrill sound penetrates your brain, then it starts beating like crazy. It was 3:15 Wednesday morning. My first thought was that Ruthanne was calling because one of my granddaughters was sick. But when I answered the phone, Mom was on the other end telling me she couldn't breathe. I told her to call 911. Throwing on some clothes, I dashed down to the car and pulled out of the garage. I'm usually pretty good about obeying speed limits, but this time I completely ignored the signs as I rushed to my mom's house, praying all the way. While speeding up the expressway, my cell phone rang. It was Steve letting me know that the paramedics had called him—they were taking Mom to the emergency room of Akron City Hospital, and I should meet them there. I beat the ambulance by several minutes. Pacing between the ER entrance and the parking lot, I continued to pray.

As they got Mom situated in a room, I took care of the insurance, etc. Several hours later we were informed that she was being admitted to the hospital. But we didn't know why—a doctor had failed to come in and let us know the reason. I had to go out into the hall to find a nurse, who then told us that Mom had pneumonia and a urinary tract infection.

After Mom was settled into a room, I drove to her house to pick up a few things that she needed. Back at the hospital, I made sure she was okay and comfortable. Then I headed home for a nap and a shower. On the way back to the hospital, my cell phone rang. It was my cousin Sally. She was visiting with my mom and said that I should get there quickly. Mom was in a crisis, having a hard time breathing. As I pulled into the parking deck, everything seemed to be moving in slow motion. Finally, inside the hospital, I hurried down the hall. Sally was standing outside Mom's room. Seeing the look on her face and the tears in her eyes, I thought for sure Mom was gone. I put my hand on my chest and started to cry. Sally rushed to my side and put her arm around me, assuring me that Mom was still with us.

When I walked into the room, I wondered if she would make it through this crisis. Mom was so pale and really struggling to breathe. The look of fear in her eyes mirrored the same look in my eyes. The doctor asked me to step out of the room so he could speak to me. They were going to transfer Mom to the intensive care unit. Her blood pressure had gone sky high. I'm so grateful that Sally was right there with me as I attempted to make sense of all he was saying. Panic set in when he said they would probably have to put her on a ventilator.

My aunt arrived, and a nurse accompanied us downstairs to a room where we could wait while they got Mom hooked up to the intravenous and oxygen. Sal had to leave to tend to her family before we were allowed in the room. After what seemed like forever, Aunt Marge and I were able to see Mom. Visiting hours were limited, so we only had a few minutes with her.

Needless to say, I spent a restless night, even though I was exhausted, both emotionally and physically. It was the next morning that I encountered the rainbow on that lonely stretch of country road.

Rainbows have been significant for me since the early years of our walk with Christ. My husband Steve and I were baptized together at an Easter sunrise service at The Chapel in 1977. When we came out of church, a double rainbow was hanging in the sky. It seemed that it was a personal message from God, conveying His pleasure in our obedience and assuring us of His promise to always be with us.

When I came across the rainbow on my way to the hospital, I again felt like God was speaking to me, confirming to my heart that all would be well. The tears that came on me so suddenly were tears of relief.

I was surprised a short time later when I walked into Mom's room. She looked like a different person than the one I left the evening before, sitting up in bed and smiling at me. Thankfully, she had stabilized, and her breathing was not as labored as it had been, so the ventilator was not needed.

A couple of days later, after she was moved to a regular room, I told Mom how scared I had been—afraid that she didn't have the strength to fight and the will to live. I knew that she was struggling with loneliness and some depression. It had only been three months since we buried my stepfather. Her words reassured me. She said she had too much to live for, much to look forward to—her great-granddaughter Audrey's second birthday party, her granddaughter Hester's wedding next April, her grandson Micah's college graduation in a few years. I very much needed to hear that determination in her voice.

Mom was released from the hospital six days after she was admitted. She spent three days at our house and then was anxious to get back to her own place. During her time with us, she signed papers on a small condo just around the corner from us. Lord willing, she will be moved in before the middle of November. I think it will be a relief for her to be close to us—I know it will be for me. We had asked her to move in with us, but she wants, and needs, a place of her own. She doesn't want what little independence she has left taken away from her. I can understand that, and I am determined to honor that for as long as possible, as long as she is able.

It's a strange feeling to have the dynamics turned around in our mother/daughter relationship. Driving her places—paying her bills—helping her make decisions—watching over her. This journey called aging can be frightening as a person struggles to adjust to physical and mental limitations. And it can sometimes be humbling—having to depend on someone else to do what you always did for yourself. Especially when that someone happens to be the child you brought into the world.

December 2005

Our God is the God of new beginnings. Even when you are 79 years old!

Without going into a lot of detail, my mother has had a troublesome life. Abuse and alcohol seem to have stalked her since she was a small child, leaving behind a trail of emotional and physical misery. Mom is such a sweet person—one who would never intentionally hurt anyone. She hardly deserved any of the pain that has been inflicted on her throughout her life. I, at times, have even felt guilt at being one of those who have brought distress to her, denying her the pleasure of watching her grandchildren grow up. I can't undo our years in the Philippines, nor would I want to. Following God's path for us, being obedient to His call on our lives, has reaped many blessings. But it has also required sacrifice. It saddens me that my mother has had to be one of those of whom sacrifice was demanded.

However, we as a family, and especially I, her daughter, have now been given the incredible opportunity to make up for some of those "lost" years, of the hands-on grandparenting she missed out on, of the family times she's been deprived of. I consider it a privilege to honor her by serving her, spending time with her, loving her, taking care of her.

As my husband Steve and I, our daughter Hester and soon to be son-in-law Dale, our son Micah, and Mom gathered around the Thanksgiving table at our house in November, I silently gave thanks to God for my family and the way He has worked throughout this year. How blessed I am! Each one of us verbally shared what we were thankful for as we ate turkey, stuffing, mashed potatoes and gravy, green bean casserole, sweet potato casserole, and rolls. That feast in itself was enough to be thankful for!

"Count your blessings—name them one by one. Count your blessings—see what God has done."

- I'm thankful that God brought us back from the Philippines when He did so that we could be here to help Mom and Paul through the ordeal of his cancer and radiation treatments. Though his death happened so much sooner than we expected, I'm grateful that Paul did not suffer long.
- I'm thankful for the birth of my granddaughter Elena Grace.
- I'm thankful for the engagement of Hester and Dale.

- I'm thankful for the birth of my granddaughter Madelyn Rose.
- I'm thankful that my mom pulled through a medical crisis.

So many, many things to be truly thankful for.

The Sunday after Thanksgiving, everyone was together at our house. Everyone except Micah, that is—he had flown back to Chicago earlier in the morning. The guys were all in the living room watching television or reading. The girls were all in the kitchen. A John Tesh CD was playing, and Sarah was singing along as she held Elena. Ruthanne was stirring adobo sauce on the stove. Audrey was getting into the cupboard with plastic bowls. Madelyn was sitting in her little chair. Hester was chopping onions. Mom was slicing tomatoes. I was cutting up chicken. An incredible sense of peace and well-being washed over me, along with a tad bit of sadness. The sadness sprang from thoughts of my childhood and missing out on having sisters or sharing mother/daughter times like I do with my daughters. But I didn't allow myself to dwell on this, because I wanted to live in the moment and relish my "Norman Rockwell" scene to the fullest. I needed to cherish this moment with my mother and daughters and granddaughters. I'm hoping there will be many more such moments, but who's to know? I don't know how much time Mom has left with us. I've prayed for so long that she would have peace in her life and that she would have the chance to enjoy her family. I'm thrilled that I am seeing this prayer answered right before my eyes!

When our kids were small, if one of us was having a bad, awful time, it was our practice to say, "let's start the day over" —even if it was right before bed. Mom has been given a fresh start in a new condo with new furniture that she deserves— living in a new community—attending a new church—meeting new friends—surrounded by her family. Is it possible to start our lives over? I do believe it is. Because our compassionate and loving God is the God of mercy and of new beginnings. Even when you are 79 years old!

January 2006

If I were in a comic strip, there would be a light bulb dangling over my head. The look on my face would be one of astonishment, because I had just made a profound discovery. A mystery had been solved. Along with that astonishment would be bewilderment at why I had not before seen what makes perfect sense to me now.

I'm referring to the paradox of feelings I have experienced while:

- gazing at a tropical sunset
- looking through my window at a snow-covered landscape
- toasting my toes in front of my fireplace

- holding my husband's hand
- quenching my thirst with a glass of ice-cold water
- driving down a country road lined with autumn trees
- watching the surf crash against the ocean shore
- cradling a grandbaby in my arms
- walking through a field of heather
- licking an ice cream cone
- sitting on the cliffs of the Irish Sea
- reading a good book
- smelling bread baking in the oven
- listening to the chatter of birds outside my bedroom window
- sniffing the fragrance of lilacs
- biting into a juicy caramel apple
- enjoying the companionship of friends
- singing songs of worship and praise
- and so much more!

Finally, I understand. Clearly, it's because I'm *homesick*. The joy or happiness I feel, coupled with a sense of sadness or pain, is simply my response to the anticipation of what's to come. When I experience all of those wonderful things, I'm getting just a glimpse of what God is preparing for those who love Him. If I'm overcome with emotion at the beauty that surrounds me here on earth, imagine how awestruck I will be when I partake of all that God has planned for me on the New Earth!

Reading Randy Alcorn's books *Heaven, In Light of Eternity* and *The Edge of Eternity* has opened new vistas for me. The thought of heaven (not the "temporary" heaven we inhabit after death, but the eternal one at the end of this age) being right here on earth—a new earth, a redeemed earth, a restored earth—a resurrected earth—just never entered my mind. I guess I always expected that we would be in a different and new place somewhere in the universe. I knew heaven would be wonderful because God would be there, but I couldn't envision what it would look like. Now I don't have to try to visualize it, because I already have a small picture of what it will be. Only it will be so much more than I can comprehend since it will be a perfect place that's free from evil and the effects of sin.

A Japanese friend of mine, Natsuko, once told me that heaven didn't sound appealing to her. She didn't particularly find streets of gold inviting—she'd much rather walk the rolling hills of Japan with the brilliant blue sky above her head and the soft green grass beneath her feet. Perhaps that's exactly what she will do!

Natsuko was a fellow missionary in the Philippines. She often was homesick for Japan just as I was homesick for the U.S. We both longed for what was familiar. It's not that we couldn't appreciate the uniqueness of Filipinos or enjoy God's creative beauty in the Philippines—it's just that it wasn't quite home—it wasn't where we belonged. Even Natsuko and I were from different parts of the world. We shared a common bond as followers of Jesus Christ and the same needs and desires as women, but we were born in different countries, ate different kinds of foods, spoke different languages, experienced different cultures. Though I had a delightful time when I visited Japan, it wasn't home. Though Natsuko lived in the U.S. for awhile, it wasn't home. Home always tugged at our heartstrings because that's where our families and our histories were.

Homesickness. I know what it feels like. Sometimes it was intense pain as if someone put his or her hand inside my chest and squeezed my heart until I couldn't breathe. Sometimes it was just a dull ache. Some days it was just a thought in the back of my mind. But it was always there.

That must be what we experience here on this old, sinful earth. Though there are so many things that bring pleasure, so much that God has blessed us with, it's not home. There's a sense of familiarity, but it's not quite home—YET! Thinking through what Randy Alcorn has written in his books, it really does make perfect sense that this earth—redeemed—will be our eternal home. After all, God proclaimed His work "good" throughout the Genesis account of creation. We're responsible for messing it up. But God isn't finished. He will one day restore the earth to its original beauty.

Whenever I would return home to Ohio from the Philippines, I always felt like a different person than the one who lived on the other side of the ocean. If that's true in this life, just imagine how much more I will be "myself" when I finally reach the home I was truly created for.

My paternal grandfather was born in Dublin, Ireland. He immigrated to the United States in the latter part of the 1800s. I never knew him. He died when my dad was only two years old. Dad loved the Irish part of his heritage. He always dreamed of visiting Ireland. Unfortunately, he died at the young age of 47 and never made that trip. I remember, though, a song that he used to sing. "If there is going to be a life hereafter, and somehow I am sure there's going to be. I will ask my God to let me make my heaven, in that dear land across the Irish Sea."

That song expresses the wistfulness we feel here and the desire of our hearts to reside eternally in a land that we love—a place where we belong. My longing for my present, "earthly home" all the years I lived somewhere else was just a shadow of what my heart truly yearns for—to dwell in the place that was made for me and, more importantly, as Adam and Eve did in the Garden, to walk with my God.

My daughter Hester and I visited Ireland during the summer of 2001. I had a chance to live one of my dreams—to sit on a cliff overlooking the Irish Sea. Maybe I'll have that chance again—in the life hereafter—with Dad sitting on one side of me and Jesus sitting on the other. Now that sounds like heaven to me! I hope I'll see you there.

February 2006

On a cold winter night a year ago, Jerry Lukens left life on this earth and entered eternity. I know that it was one of the most difficult days that his wife, Dorla, ever lived through. I'd like to use my sanctified imagination, as Randy Alcorn calls it in his book *Heaven*, to imagine what Jerry might have experienced on that evening. I have Dorla's permission to do so.

> Jerry.
> Is that You, Lord?
> Yes, Jerry.
> It's time, Lord, isn't it?
> Yes it is, Jerry. It's time to come home to Me.
> But, Lord, I've fought so hard to live. I don't want to leave Dorla yet. I love her so much. I'm worried about her.
> Oh Jerry, I know you are. But she'll be okay. Don't forget—I love her more than you could ever love her. She's my precious child, and I will always be with her. And I have placed My children in her life, to surround her with love and care.
> Yes, Lord. I know. The day we walked into Mike's ABF was providential. You were working even through that, Lord, because You knew what was ahead for us. You were already preparing for this day, weren't You?
> Yes, I was, Jerry. I knew that Dorla would need these people in her life. But I also knew that these dear ones would need Dorla in their lives. I still have work for Dorla to do. She must be about My kingdom business. There will be many happenings in the next several months that will require her prayers and her

compassion. Why, she doesn't know it yet, but she will have a girls' slumber party at your house for one of my treasured daughters—a birthday party for Lois. You know Lois is suffering with breast cancer. She needs to be encouraged by the women in your ABF. What fun they will have that night!

Lord? My house filled with giggling women? Oh my.

Yes, Jerry. I love to see my daughters enjoying themselves. It's not just Lois, though, Jerry. Dorla will be on her knees many times. And she will extend kindness and tenderness to those who need it. There will be much pain in the coming year. Bruce and Joni will carry a heavy burden dealing with Matt's illness. Gary and Beth will go through a difficult time when lightning strikes their house, causing it to catch on fire. Marie will struggle with the stress of raising children, working, and going to school. Mary's stepfather will die in June, after battling cancer. Dorla's friendship will be a comfort to her. And this is really exciting. Mary's mother will start to attend church, and Dorla will reach out to her. So much will happen in your absence, Jerry. Amy will need her mother as she goes through some painful times. Fran will shed tears over her father's cancer. Daniel will have a dangerous encounter with a deer—his life will be spared, partially due to Dorla's prayers for him. Rebecca will have a tough time in her relationship with her son. People will endure physical pain—Karyn, Marie, Joyce, Keith, Ayesha, Bunny. Some will need surgery—Jim, Beth, Barb, Bruce. Many will lose loved ones—Shirley, Gary, Karl, Connie. But there will also be some happy and exciting events. Lots of new grandchildren. Weddings and engagements of children. Dorla will rejoice right along with them.

Some will be faced with making big decisions—like Marty and Jeanne—major changes are coming their way. And then there's Lois. I will heal Lois in answer to the prayers of Dorla and all those who have prayed. There's still so much to do. So many that will need Dorla's ministry. You can see, Jerry, that I have much work for Dorla to do before I call her home.

I can see that, Lord. I've already told her she needs to carry on—that she has work to do. It will still be hard for her, though. I know her. There will be tears. Nights will be lonely.

Yes, Jerry. There will be much heart-wrenching grief for her to deal with. I will be there to comfort her. And I'll help her to remember the wonderful years she's had with you. She has much to be thankful for. Mary will say it well at your memorial service in a few days. She'll remind Dorla that I blessed you both with an amazing love.

It was amazing, Lord. I loved her so much. I still do.

Of course you do, Jerry. I wouldn't want that to change just because you won't be physically with her. Love transcends all time and space. My love lasts forever.

Thank You, Lord, that it lasts forever.

We've talked enough for now, Jerry. Take My hand. I'm ready for you to come home.

And I'm ready to be with You, Lord. It's been a long battle, and I'm weary. But I will miss my beautiful wife.

It's only for a season, Jerry. She'll be here with you before you know it.

Goodbye, Dorla. I'll be waiting to welcome you home. While we are apart, I'll be helping the Lord with your mansion. Since we've already built a house together, I know exactly what you like.

With a bit of sadness because of what he was leaving behind, but also with great anticipation at what was ahead, Jerry said, "Okay, Lord. Let's go."

As Jerry slipped through the curtain of eternity, he found himself face to face with his Savior. He was so overwhelmed with the majesty and magnificence of the Lord that he fell to his knees—bowing in worship and crying tears of joy. The only word that could be heard escaping his lips was that Name above all names—Jesus.

The Lord lifted Jerry to his feet and tenderly gathered him into His safe and strong arms. He spoke softly:

> Welcome My good and faithful servant. I am pleased with your life, Jerry, for you have touched many hearts on your journey—many of them through your most difficult days. I know there is more that you wanted to do, but you have accomplished all that I planned for you. Through your pain, everyone saw your faith and marveled at your courage. You were determined that you would not be defeated. And you were not! Death was not a threat to you, for even as cancer ravaged your body, you kept your eyes focused on Me. You did not give up. You did not become bitter. Instead, you embraced the suffering. Enter now, My son, into the joy and happiness of your Master. Welcome home, My beloved, Jerry.

March 2006

A lazy morning found me rummaging through a box of papers I had brought back from the Philippines. A box full of memories—both good and bad. One paper caught my eye. It was something I wrote several years ago during a particularly difficult time in my life. I didn't know if I wanted to revisit the feelings of turmoil I saw in the first few lines, but I read it anyway. I'm glad I did. If life is weighing you down, if the storms are fierce, the struggles severe, I open my heart to you once more, praying that my words of yesterday might encourage you today and help you to realize that, though we are surrounded by intense spiritual warfare, our God is mighty and powerful and strong—and He's on our side!

My life is a battle.
   My enemy is myself.
A war rages inside of my head.
   The battlefield is my heart,
      where my thoughts wreak havoc with my emotions,
         causing self-inflicted wounds to my soul;
      emotions exploding like grenades,
         or like tripping across minefields,
            triggering unexpected explosions.
Conflicts by day.
Terror by night.

Weary of the ups and downs of
   short-lived mountaintop victories
      low-valley defeats.
Longing to walk on level ground.
Hot.
Dusty.
Tired.
Thirsty.

My eyes see…only ME.

David sang words that could have been my own.

"Be merciful to me, O LORD, for I am in distress; my eyes grow weak with sorrow, my soul and my body with grief. My life is consumed by anguish and my years by groaning; my strength fails because of my affliction, and my bones grow weak" (Psalm 31:9–10).

"I am bowed down and brought very low; all day long I go about mourning. My back is filled with searing pain; there is no health in my body. I am feeble and utterly crushed; I groan in anguish of heart. All my longings lie open before You, O Lord; my sighing is not hidden from you. My heart pounds, my strength fails me; even the light has gone from my eyes" (Psalm 38:6–10).

I read the Psalms through the watches of the night.

Then I know.
I am *not* the enemy!
There is one outside of myself that taunts and attacks, who wishes to destroy me.
At times I succumb to Satan's tactics,
allowing him to invade my thoughts,
but …

"Be strong in the Lord and in His mighty power. Put on the full armor of God so that you can take your stand against the devil's schemes. For our struggle is not against flesh and blood, but against the rulers, against the authorities, against the powers of this dark world and against the spiritual forces of evil in the heavenly realms. Therefore put on the full armor of God, so that when the day of evil comes, you may be able to stand your ground, and after you have done everything, to stand. Stand firm then, with the belt of truth buckled around your waist, with the breastplate of righteousness in place, and with your feet fitted with the readiness that comes from the gospel of peace. In addition to all this, take up the shield of faith, with which you can extinguish all the flaming arrows of the evil one. Take the helmet of salvation and the sword of the Spirit, which is the Word of God. And pray in the Spirit on all occasions with all kinds of prayers and requests" (Ephesians 6:10–18).

I remember.
THE BATTLE BELONGS TO THE LORD.
HE has given me everything I need to defend myself.
The victory is already HIS.

I had cried out to my LORD, and HE heard me.
HE is my tower of refuge and strength, and my soul finds rest in HIM.

HE wiped the tears from my eyes,
　　clearing my blurred and distorted "vision";
　　　　and now

My eyes see—only HIM.

April 2006

The living room of our small apartment was quiet on an evening in December 1971. I had no siblings to keep me company. My dad had died three-and-a-half years earlier. My mom was out. She still found it difficult to be at home where she had to deal with her grief and loneliness. My boyfriend Steve was at work. As I sat on the couch watching television, feeling utterly alone, a movie came on that touched the lonely places in my heart—*The Homecoming*. It was about a family—grandfather, grandmother, father, mother, and seven children—who lived in the Blue Ridge Mountains of Virginia. I fell in love with that family. A series spun off from the movie several months later, and every Thursday evening found me engrossed in the daily lives of these characters. I felt at home in their house. I entered into their love for each other. I cried when *John Boy* left home to move to New York. I laughed when *Grandpa* teased *Grandma*. I rejoiced when *Mary Ellen* gave birth to *John Curtis*. I wept when *Grandpa Walton* died. What they experienced, I experienced. *The Waltons* became my family, so much so that when the series ended, I grieved as if I had lost another loved one.

I still watch re-runs of *The Waltons*, but with a different mindset from that young woman of long ago. She could never have imagined the direction her life would take and how the lonely places in her heart would be filled:

- salvation and eternal life through Jesus Christ
- marriage to my high school sweetheart
- births of four wonderful children
- opportunity to live and serve God for many years in a foreign country
- high school graduations of all my children
- college graduations of my three daughters (my son has one more year)
- weddings of two daughters (adding two sons-in-law)
- births of three beautiful granddaughters
- my mother living close by
- house in Hartville
- ministry at The Chapel.

There have been, of course, times of sadness and difficulty sprinkled among these blessings. That's all part of life—all part of what has molded me into the woman I am today—a woman whose heart is overflowing!

Miraculously, this full heart of mine has room to expand as our family grows by two this year.

Our daughter will marry on April 8, giving us a new son-in-law.

And in October, our daughter Sarah and son-in-law Brandon will give us a new grandchild!

Mom and I flew to Virginia for a visit a few weeks ago. Sarah showed us around their two-bedroom apartment (they were still in a one-bedroom apartment the last time I was there). "This is Elena's room," Sarah said as we walked into the cute bedroom decorated with Winnie the Pooh. "And this …" pointing at the cradle in her and Brandon's room "…is the new baby's bed." What? New baby? Oh my gosh, I'm going to be a grandmother again!

Elena and her brother or sister will be just 17 months apart. Sarah will definitely need her mother within reach. Right? Oh good—maybe this means they will be moving back to Ohio! Wrong! Wishful thinking. By the time the baby comes along, they may be even further away than Virginia. Try *Denver, Colorado!* "Lord, You don't really mean for them to take my grandchildren so far away, do You? Oh yeah. Right. I forgot. I did that same thing, didn't I? But this is different! Isn't it? Lord, please open up a job opportunity for Brandon in Northeast Ohio that he cannot refuse. After all, this move to Denver is not a done deal yet. Hmm. I know, Lord. I'm being selfish. I really do want Your best for them, even if that does mean a move to Colorado. Okay, but I don't like it. Long-distance grandparenting is for the birds!"

I actually had that conversation with the Lord. There's nothing more I would love than to have all my family near me. I tend to think that I'm the only one who knows what's best for us, but God has proven His love and sovereignty in our lives time and time again. He is the Wise One who has and who will shepherd my family, seeing each of our futures through His eternal eyes. He is faithful and will accomplish His purposes for every one of us—whether in Ohio, Virginia, or Colorado.

This morning I sat on the couch in the quiet living room of my house—not the one where my TV family lived on *Waltons Mountain*, but the one where my real family lives in the Village of Hartville. As my husband kissed me goodbye before he left for work, I turned on the television to "visit" with that fictitious family from my past. I enjoyed watching the episode, but realized that I haven't needed the *Waltons* for a very long time. God has filled the lonely places of my heart—something that only He could do—gifting me with a family—a family that has gone through trials and transitions and separations; a family that has laughed together, played together, prayed together, cried together, rejoiced together; a family that has a lifetime of stories to tell and precious memories to treasure. A family that always has and always will be knit together with love—no matter how many miles might separate us.

"For everything you have missed, you have gained something else." (Ralph Waldo Emerson)

May 2006

We were sitting on my bed, my daughter and I, as I sang *Goodnight, My Love* to her one last time on the eve of her wedding day. Steve and I sang the same song to her and her sisters and brother every night when they were growing up. It was the song I sang to Sarah on the night before her wedding day and to Ruthanne on the night before her wedding day. This time it was Hester's turn.

The house was filled with girls—six of Hester's classmates from Faith Academy in the Philippines. They came from Virginia, Pennsylvania, California, and as far away as Australia to share in the joyous occasion with their friend. It was a wonderful reunion. Some of them had not seen each other since graduation in 1998.

I needed a few minutes of privacy with my daughter, so we retreated to my bedroom. We talked, and then I sang to her. And we cried. My tears were a mixture of many emotions, but mostly joy. My little girl was getting married in the morning!

The next day dawned a bit overcast, but the sun popped through the clouds as the ceremony drew near. We bustled about getting ready, and then it was time to take our seats. The bridesmaids walked in, followed by the junior bridesmaids. Then my adorable granddaughter Audrey, just two-and-a-half years old, preceded the bride. Prompted by her Uncle Micah, she walked into the room, dropping her rose petals in just a couple of clumps, determined to accomplish her task as flower girl quickly!

The moment had arrived—my daughter on the arm of her father—a radiant and beautiful bride! At the front stood her groom, ready to receive his bride. Love shone bright in their eyes.

Hester's best friend's father performed the ceremony. John and his family had been like a second family to Hester, especially during her college years when we were so far away. Halfway through the wedding, Hester had arranged for Filipino traditions, just as her sisters did in their weddings. Steve explained the traditions as Sarah and Ruthanne pinned the veil and draped the cord over the bride and groom.... Then exchanging of the vows... exchanging of the rings...the proclamation that Hester and Dale were man and wife...a kiss...Mr. and Mrs. Dale Dailey!

Lunch followed, and we had opportunity to chat with the guests. Dale's brother Scott then stood to give the toast. After a few funny stories, he told us about when he had asked Dale how he knew that Hester was the one. Dale answered him that Hester was the only woman that he had ever been able to be vulnerable with. Scott thanked Hester for breaking down the wall that Dale had built, allowing him to share his feelings, at least with her. I was holding my husband's hand at the time. Steve let go to reach into his pocket for his handkerchief—we were both so touched by what Scott said.

Dale then stood as his bride sat at the table. He said that Hester was a gift to him—a gift of love. He then spoke of the amazing gift of love that both he and Hester had received— salvation and faith in Jesus Christ. His groomsmen each read a portion of Scripture. We were greatly impressed with the courage of this young man to stand up in front of family and friends to proclaim the beliefs which he and Hester shared. As I observed all of this, something significant occurred to me. I don't know if it was intentionally planned, but this is the picture I got. Because Hester sat at the table while Dale stood to talk, it seemed to me the perfect portrayal of a wife submitting the spiritual leadership to her husband—just as God ordained marriage to be.

The reception continued as Hester tossed the bridal bouquet in the air. It landed on the floor and was picked up by her best friend, Rachel. The bride and groom then cut the wedding cake and were very respectful as they gave each other a bite of the delicious cake which, by the way, was made by my son-in-law Brandon!

Months of planning, and it was all over. But what a fantastic memory to add to our family history. Such a lovely day. A simple, yet elegant wedding. We had prayed that the Lord would be honored throughout, and we feel that He most certainly was. And we are confident that He will continue to be honored through the lives of this precious couple—my daughter and her new husband.

June 2006

The rain was falling softly on the lake, creating gentle ripples on the surface. Seabirds were gliding overhead. I was warm and cozy lying in the recliner next to the fireplace. The sound of giggling women came from the kitchen. They were having a great time experimenting with make-up while a Mary Kay consultant gave them tips. I was not participating because of the lingering affects of a cold. Instead, my body was relaxing as my eyelids drooped in drowsiness. It felt so good to let go of the cares of life.

The weekend event was a gathering of missionary women. We had served all over the world: Eastern Europe, Asia, Southeast Asia, Africa. Different seasons of life. Different seasons of service—one very close to leaving for her first term—me back home now after four terms.

We were staying at the beautiful guest house on Portage Lakes that friends had created just for missionaries. A haven. A safe place.

The sense of safety came not just from being in this incredible house, though. It really came from being in the company of women—women who understood, who had shared similar experiences—who had been there, done that. Some of us were battle-scarred. Some of us were still in the healing process. All of us were able to acknowledge God's goodness and His faithfulness in our lives. All of us were thankful for His grace that saw us through challenges and transitions—grateful for the opportunities to serve Him and grow in a foreign land.

The evening before, as we ate pizza and salad for supper, we shared together the highs and lows of our lives—each with a different story to tell. Afterwards, we went downstairs to the family room, clad in our jammies, and laughed together as we watched a funny international movie.

Whether we are talking, sitting in silence, playing, laughing, crying, or praying—there's a level of understanding and empathy among missionary women that many other women might not be able to relate to. Sometimes all it takes is a look or a word, and we know. We just know. We know what she's going through because there seems to be an invisible tie that binds us together.

Lest you think this is an exclusive club, let me guarantee you that membership is open—not to just those who are willing to go, but to those who are willing to stay—to stay put and be part of the team here at home. Acts 21:5–6 says, "When our time was up, we left and continued on our way. All the disciples and their wives and children accompanied us out of the city, and there on the beach we knelt to pray. After saying goodbye to each other, we went aboard the ship, *and they returned home.*" (Emphasis mine.)

Membership requirements are:

1. You must be a WOMAN. Only a woman can understand the roller coaster emotions and raging hormones!
2. You must be a PRAY-er. This is crucial for it's where the real battle takes place.
3. You must be a LISTENER. Every missionary needs someone to listen to her stories, to hear what she has to say.
4. You must be GRACIOUS. A missionary needs someone to share her disappointments, heartaches, and trials with—without being judged—someone who understands that missionary women are human and don't belong on the pedestal on which they are often placed.
5. You must be BOLD. We all need someone to be accountable with—someone who will tell us the hard "stuff" in love.
6. You must be TRUSTWORTHY. Confidentiality is extremely important.

I was privileged to have a "Circle of Women" here at home who surrounded me while I was in the Philippines. They prayed when I most needed it. They listened to what I had to say. They didn't judge me but accepted me for who I was. They told me things I didn't want to hear but needed to hear.

Now I have the honor of being the stay-at-home part of another "Circle of Women." (Please note that I have Joanie's permission to share this.) God connected me with Joanie through e-mail while I was still in the Philippines. She and her husband were preparing to go out to the Philippines for their first term. A mutual friend, Becky, brought us together. When Joanie first e-mailed me with questions about life in this Southeast Asian nation, I asked her how honest she wanted me to be. Her desire was to hear the whole truth—good and bad. Thus began a wonderful friendship. Fortunately, Steve and I were still in the country when Joanie and Will arrived, so we had the opportunity to meet them face-to-face and briefly show them around parts of Manila. What a unique couple! And fun. Boy do I have some stories to tell! One of the first things I noticed was a twinkle, a sparkle in Joanie's eyes which revealed her zest for life. She was a woman who was thrilled to finally be in the Philippines serving her Lord.

How well I remember coming home after our first four-year term—weary emotionally, physically, and spiritually. The stress of culture shock, homesickness, language learning, illnesses, relationships, and more caused overwhelming exhaustion. Will and Joanie came home last year feeling the effects of cross-cultural ministry. They experienced some very difficult trials, as well as hard disappointments. Becky and her husband invited us, along with four other couples, to their house to meet with Will and Joanie and to hear of their passion for the Filipino people. One of the first things I noticed was that the sparkle was missing from Joanie's eyes. And I knew, I just knew that this dear sister was hurting.

Becky was aware of my prayer circle, so a few days later when we talked at church, she mentioned how wonderful it would be if Joanie could have a "Circle of Women" who prayed for her. Knowing first hand what an encouragement it is to have the support of friends, I was determined that Joanie would have this before she returned to the Philippines several months later. All the women who met at Becky's house earlier showed a real interest in Joanie and her ministry, so we decided these could potentially be the ones to surround her with love and care. I got busy making phone calls. Each one was more than willing—they were excited to be part of this missionary's "Circle of Women."

We had our first meeting at my house. We talked about the need for confidentiality—the need for graciousness—the need for boldness—the need for fervent prayer. Thankfulness doesn't adequately describe what Joanie felt knowing that a group of Christian sisters were willing to do this for her. She was overwhelmed with gratitude and humility. She even gave our circle a name. The 142:7 Women—taken from Psalm 142, verse 7: "Your people will form a circle around me and you'll bring me showers of blessing!" I love it!

We had our last meeting at Becky's house the night before Will and Joanie left to return to the Philippines. One of the first things I noticed was that the sparkle was back in Joanie's eyes!

July 2006

They're all gone. A whole generation. My dad and his siblings. No one to answer the questions I have. No one to fill in the blanks. No one to tell the stories of grandparents or great-grandparents.

I've tried doing some genealogy research online with the help of my son, but that can only provide general facts. My computer can't tell me if I resemble a great-grandmother. It doesn't have the ability to show me what my dad was like as a child. It won't reveal skeletons in my family's closet. It is unable to tell me the story of how my grandparents met. It refuses to answer the questions I have about my dad's experiences during World War II.

My father served his country in the same islands where I served my God for so many years. I often walked the streets of Manila with Dad in my thoughts—realizing that he could have walked those very same streets. I would close my eyes and try to imagine what Manila was like back then. What did he see? What were his thoughts? Was he homesick? What was it that he experienced that made him always disappear in later years at Fourth of July picnics, just as the fireworks started? Had he been frightened, traumatized? I don't know.

He was a quiet man, my dad. He never spoke of the war. Even if he had opened up before he died, as a young girl I probably wouldn't have been particularly interested. There were more "important" things to occupy my teenage mind. How I wish I would have taken the time to sit and talk with him. I wish that we would have had more time together so that I could have known him as an adult. Why is it that those longings to know about the past don't happen until we're older, after it may be too late to find answers? Why do we even feel compelled to examine our histories, to delve into the past? Would it really help us to understand ourselves better— to define who we are?

Here's a thought—could it be a yearning that God placed within our hearts? Perhaps some day in eternity He'll provide all the answers we're looking for. I can only speculate, but maybe I'll have the chance to open up a book and read all about my family history. Better yet, maybe I'll have the opportunity to sit with a relative and hear first hand the stories that I've missed here on earth. I can't help but think that our relationships, our experiences, our histories not only mold us into the people we are here, but also will affect who we are in the life to come. I refuse to believe that God will erase from our minds all that happened to us during the course of our earthly lives. Will being in the presence of the Lord dissipate the need or desire to know what took place in centuries past? On the contrary, I think the desire will be even stronger, because we will be face-to-face with the Author of history. As we read or watch or however He chooses to reveal our family stories, we will marvel at how He worked in our lives and the lives of our parents, grandparents, great-grandparents, and back through our family trees. We will praise Him even more when we realize the extent of what He has done for us beyond salvation and eternal life. Yes, these are the most important elements of His grace and mercy, but just think of how our hearts will overflow with love for Jesus when we fully understand how that grace and mercy were woven throughout the generations and how He patterned our lives. I would not be who I am today if my grandfather had not left Ireland, settled in Pennsylvania, and married my grandmother. I'd be a completely different person.

At a Pastors' Wives meeting recently, we discussed unfinished personal projects. Mine was a family story/scrapbook.

I shared a passage from *A Step Farther and Higher* by Gail MacDonald. The author talked about taking the time to write down our blessings and our trials, the high moments of our lives and the low moments, the beauty and the pain. Some day, when our children read our journals, they will see how God worked in our lives. Our journeys will give them courage as they realize how much God's grace saw us through the difficult times.

My story/scrapbook is a work in progress—not only do I have to write about the past, but I have to keep up with the present. I do this because I want my children and grandchildren and great-grandchildren to see and know and learn from what I have to say so that they will not have to guess at what our family was about. I want them to have something tangible in front of them so that they can read about the God of their father and mother, grandfather and grandmother, great-grandfather and great-grandmother. I desire that they have the advantage of knowing here what the Lord did in our lives and not have to wait or guess or question, because it could affect how they live and where they spend eternity. Deuteronomy 4:9 in the *New Living Translation* says, "Watch out! Be very careful never to forget what you have seen the Lord do for you. Do not let these things escape from your mind as long as you live! And be sure to pass them on to your children and grandchildren." As Gail MacDonald implied, Steve and I want those who come behind us to find courage for their own journey when they realize how much a God of grace empowered our climb. The lyrics of a Steve Green song speak what's in our hearts:

Oh may all who come behind us find us faithful.

October 2006

I surprised my husband with tickets to a Michael Card concert in July. Michael is one of Steve's favorite recording artists/songwriters. If you know Steve, you can guess the reason. It's because Michael sings from the Scriptures. And if you do know Steve, you know how important the Word of God is to him.

We had dinner out together and then went on to the First Friends Church in North Canton. The concert was fantastic! There was one particular song that really captured my attention:

"Older Than the Rain"

In the song, the artist tells us that Human tears are older than the rain. Mankind has been crying tears of sorrow and pain since Adam and Eve were banished from the Garden of Eden. I have a hunch that it was probably Eve who experienced the first tears. Did she weep when she realized that God's presence was no longer there and she was to blame? Sob when she was forced to move away from "home" to a strange place? Whine when she and Adam had their first argument? Moan through the pangs of childbirth? Wail in grief when her son was murdered by his brother?

I wonder—has anything much really changed since Eve walked this earth? Solomon said that there is nothing new under the sun. We are still crying. And we will continue to cry until the day when our Savior wipes every tear from our eyes. Until that time, we wade through the pain. How do we do it? How can we get through the anguish without being buried alive? There are people, friends, in my life right now who are going through intense struggles and afflictions. My heart hurts for them so much. My tears mingle with theirs.

There have been moments in my own life when I've almost passed out from physical pain; seasons when I thought I would suffocate from the agony of emotional suffering; times when I felt like I was drowning in spiritual misery—all of these accompanied by oceans of tears. Psalm 56:8 says, "You keep track of all my sorrows. You have collected all my tears in Your bottle. You have recorded each one in Your book" (*New Living Translation*). Surely the bottle with my name on it is overflowing.

Today I was running errands in the dreary autumn weather, rain splashing against my windshield. A song was playing on the radio. The words reflected a hopelessness that would be easy for any of us to succumb to: about the world being full of fear and people being in confusion, wondering if anyone cares, hearing the people crying.

Can anybody hear? Does anybody care? Where is the hope they long for? I hear the people crying. Talk about depressing! To keep myself from diving headlong into a black mood, I put a Casting Crowns CD in the player: I will praise You in this storm.

Well, not a particularly uplifting song to calm my troubled heart. But it conveys what the other song doesn't—a hope, an assurance that Someone hears, Someone cares. And if I listen, really listen, I will hear His Holy Spirit whisper to my soul: "I am with you." That's it—that's how we are able to walk, or crawl, day-by-day, or sometimes moment-by-moment through the trials, through gut-wrenching grief, through overwhelming suffering, remembering that Jesus is with us. He joins us on our journey. He never leaves our side. His enabling, all-sufficient grace is always there. Jesus holds in His hand every tear that mankind has cried.

If my heart aches for those around me who are suffering, imagine how much more He who is Perfect Love feels their pain, feels my pain. *I felt every teardrop when in darkness you cried, and I strove to remind you that for those tears I died.*

Can we, will we, after all He has done for us, lift our hands, and though our hearts are torn, praise Him in the storms?

November 2006

Snow lightly fell as I backed out of the driveway. My husband Steve stood at the front door waving goodbye. I was driving to Virginia for the birth of our fourth grandchild. Several months ago I thought I might be flying to Colorado for this joyous occasion. God must have heard the cry of this grandmother's heart. He kept my daughter Sarah, son-in-law Brandon, and granddaughter Elena a bit closer to home.

I had a long drive ahead of me. Since I wasn't really in a hurry, I decided to enjoy myself and revel in the autumn landscape. A few minutes after I reached the Allegheny Valley in Pennsylvania, the clouds parted, and the sun broke out. Ohhh! The trees were ablaze with vibrant colors! A flock of what seemed to be a hundred birds flew overhead, migrating south for the winter. The Casting Crowns Christian group was singing on the CD player: telling me that God is worthy of all our honor, glory, and praise. God's brilliant majesty was evident in His gorgeous creation around me, and I couldn't help but worship Him!

Just as quickly as the sun shone through, it disappeared behind the clouds, and the snow started falling again. The higher I climbed in the hills, the harder the snow came down. The trees and grass were covered with a thin layer of white. It was time for a break, so I stopped at the next rest plaza. I couldn't believe how cold it was as I filled the gas tank. I hurried inside to warm up. More snow had fallen while I enjoyed a Café Mocha from Starbucks. The windshield actually needed to be brushed off when I came out. Unbelievable! It was only October 24—it shouldn't have been that cold. No matter. I cranked up the heat and cranked up the volume on the CD player. Soon the heater had warmed my hands and feet, and the music had warmed my heart.

What really warmed my heart, though, was walking through the door of the Klingler apartment a few hours later and seeing my oldest daughter heavy with child. And then to hear my precious granddaughter call me Grandma for the first time. Is it any wonder that my heart melted?!

The next morning found me pacing the exact same hospital hallways that I had walked 16 ½ months earlier when Elena was born. Pacing…and waiting…waiting…waiting…until I heard the familiar voice of my son-in-law. "Grandma, do you want to see your new grandson?" Jumping up out of the chair, where I was trying to concentrate on reading, I exclaimed, "Are you serious?! It's a *boy*?" I hugged Brandon, and with tears clouding my vision, I took my first peek at my *grandson*. My grandson! He was so perfect and so beautiful! I stood at the nursery window for the longest time, gazing lovingly and with misty eyes at this newest addition to our family. My heart expanded yet once again.

Paul Steven. Named after his grandfathers. Paul means little one. Steven means crown. Proverbs 17:6 says, "Grandchildren are the crowning glory of the aged." I pray that this little one will not only be a crowning glory to his grandparents, but also that he would be a reflection of God's glory.

I spent ten days with my Virginia family—ten days of pure joy. Playing with my granddaughter, giggling, tickling her tummy with "Grandma's tickle bug," kissing her chubby cheeks, whispering in her ear, "Grandma loves you," reading her books, singing, "Oh sweet pea, won't you be my girl?", going for walk-a-walks and telling her that "God made the trees, God made the flowers." Cuddling my grandson, rocking him, kissing his soft dimpled cheeks (yes, he has dimples!), whispering in his ear, "Grandma loves you," inhaling his sweet baby fragrance.

And yes, the day did come when I had to say goodbye. It was time for Grandma Bucy to go home to Grandpa Bucy and time to let Grandma K get in on the fun. I drove off not only with tears streaming down my face and a sadness in my heart, but also with a smile on my face and a delight filling my heart. Thank You, Lord Jesus!

December 2006

It was "Christmas in July." The hall was decorated in red, green, white, and gold. A trimmed Christmas tree stood off to the side. Christmas music played in the background until the noise reached a level where it could no longer be heard. The turnout of guests was better than I had anticipated. Cousins we hadn't seen in years. Old friends from the past. New friends from the present. All gathered together to honor a woman—a baby girl born on a cold Christmas Eve in 1926.

She walked into the room expecting to help set up for a surprise party for her granddaughter and grandson-in-law. Instead, she encountered a room full of people shouting out, "SURPRISE!" Confusion and bewilderment were evident on her face until I whispered in her ear: "The party is for you, Mom."

She was overcome with emotion, tears streaming down her face as she finally realized that indeed the surprise party was for her.

We were celebrating my mother's 80th birthday. Even though she will not turn 80 until December 24 of this year, we chose to have the party in the summer, when more people were likely to attend—and at a time when she certainly wouldn't be suspicious.

Because of her Hungarian heritage, we served pigs-in-the-blanket (cabbage rolls) with mashed potatoes, chicken paprikash with dumplings, and sausage.

It was a wonderful evening—a memorable one—one I know that Mom will never forget. She seemed to cry throughout the entire party. Every time another person walked up to talk with her, her eyes would well up with tears. In fact, she was still crying three days later! It astonished her that anyone would do this for her. She shared with me that no one had ever had a party for her before. Can you imagine? Almost 80 years old and never having anyone celebrate you in such a fashion! It made me sad. Of course, we went to her house every December 24 for her birthday. And she said that her sisters gave her a baby shower when she was carrying me— but that was 55 years ago!

I'm so glad we had this special celebration for a special woman in my life. I encourage you today to honor and celebrate someone you care about. Before it's too late.

January 2007

Five-and-a-half months after we celebrated my mother's 80th birthday with an early surprise party, a more significant celebration took place. My husband had the privilege of baptizing Mom at the Christmas Eve morning worship service! Our son, daughters, sons-in-law, and three cousins were present, as well as many members of our Adult Bible Fellowship. Steve introduced his mother-in-law and mentioned that it was her 80th birthday. The congregation applauded at this milestone. Then he asked her family and friends to stand. Not only did all stand in the five pews we had reserved, but there were others sprinkled throughout the auditorium who supported my mom by standing with us. There was an audible "Ohhhhh!" from the congregation. Steve asked her a few questions concerning her faith in Jesus Christ and then attempted to baptize her. I say attempted because it took him a couple of tries to actually get her dunked! Her legs wouldn't cooperate, and Steve struggled to get her under the water. There was a bit of chuckling in the room, until she was finally immersed and then raised up—symbolic of her dying to her sins and being raised up in newness of life in Christ! My heart was full of joy as I observed this public declaration of faith!

After the service, I went up to our worship pastor and hugged him, thanking him for making it possible for us to have the baptism on Christmas Eve. He thought it was great and said that it was like everyone in the auditorium had adopted Mom as their own mother!

So much has happened to my mother since she was widowed for a second time in June 2005. In November of the same year she started attending The Chapel with us, just after she moved to a condo in Hartville that was around the corner from our house. She has been exposed to so many new and wonderful things. As she sat under the teaching of the Word of God week after week, I was eager for her to understand the Bible and the depth of God's love for her. Despite my well-meaning eagerness to explain biblical truth and doctrine to her, I still fretted about just how much she would be able to comprehend. My husband in wisdom answered my anxieties with, "Mary, I am convinced that all we need to do is love her with the love of Jesus."

Casting Crowns sings a song with that very same message:

Just love her like Jesus, carry her to Him.

Love her like Jesus. That's just what we have done. And she has responded. Not just to our love, but also the love that our Growing Together ABF has lavished on her. God's love is *so powerful!* My mom is living proof, just as I am, that His love has the power to change lives. She had been battered and bruised emotionally, her spirit broken, but now she is learning to experience and accept the forgiveness, healing, freedom, and peace that come only through the grace and mercy of our Savior.

A few days before Mom's baptism, Steve and I were lying in bed talking about the amazing changes we saw in her. Others had recently commented to us that they, too, had seen a transformation. Steve rolled over and said something so profound that I had to get out of bed to write it down. He said, "Her soul is waking up." Wow!

Hallelujah!

12/24/2006

February 2007

On the drive back home from Virginia in November, I stopped in Pennsylvania to visit a friend that I hadn't seen for several years. Over a Pumpkin Latte we caught up on each other's lives. During our conversation, my friend mentioned that she had been challenged lately to "think outside the box."

That statement has popped into my head often in the past months. What does it mean to "think outside the box"? I asked a few friends for their opinions. This is what Susie said: "To me it is the freedom to do and think differently than the norm. It is stretching myself and others to get below the obvious and trivial. It is risky and scary at times, because most people are swimming upstream and you are swimming down. It is admitting to and allowing for the reality of uniqueness and individuality that may or may not fit in with the way others are. It is courage to have passions and dreams that others think are impossible or ridiculous. It is standing tall against the strong pressure to act, speak, dress, behave, and think like everyone else. It is the freedom to skip when others are walking…to speak when others are silent…to try when the crowd says it can't be done."

I've known Susie for many years. Her husband and mine were pastoral interns together at The Chapel back in the 80s. She's been through some tremendous pain in her life. I remember sitting on the steps of our porch with her shortly after attending the funeral of her precious baby daughter, my heart aching for her. Several years later we had lunch together at Luigi's, where we talked about our first term of missionary service in the Philippines and about their new adventure of starting a church in Kent, Ohio—a challenge that she took on with excitement and trepidation. And now Susie and Paul have come full circle, just as we have, and are back on staff at The Chapel. She has a real heart for women, especially pastors' wives. In the short time that she has been with us, she has encouraged and challenged me. I have so appreciated her honesty and transparency. I say this with great respect and admiration—Susie lives outside the box!

Thinking outside of the box can be exciting, exhilarating, scary, sometimes stressful, and often frustrating. Susie knows this. And I know because we were forced to think, and live, outside the box—our American culture box—when we went to the Philippines in 1986. Life the way we knew it changed radically the moment we stepped off the plane. We moved out of our comfort zone and were suddenly aliens in a foreign land.

It was necessary to process our thoughts through a whole new grid. But not just one new grid—we had to sort through several, as our mission organization was comprised of Americans, Canadians, Germans, Chinese, Australians, and Japanese. There were even contrasts within the American contingent, as we came from different parts of the U.S.—from Maine to Ohio to California—and various states in between.

Our pre-field orientation had prepared us to view many aspects of Philippine culture as different—not good or bad—just different from our own. Of course, we also had to be aware of those values or practices which were not biblical—always examining through the lens of Scripture. We openly admit that there were times when the culture rubbed us the wrong way, when it was irritating. Cultural differences occasionally led to misunderstandings and conflict. We had to learn to alter the way we responded in order not to offend. Adapting to a new culture was time-consuming, as well as exhausting, and we often had to remind ourselves why we were there. Many days I wanted to crawl back into my "American" box.

All of these adjustments had to be made without totally losing sight of who we were. We were Americans who would one day return to our country. Even though we gained a greater appreciation for Filipinos, we would never be Filipinos. This certainly made life an interesting challenge, albeit a difficult one at times.

Sandy M., a fellow missionary in the Philippines, wrote, "Understanding cultural differences is crucial, but this understanding must be combined with love and a desire to pursue unity." What joy we experienced when we put aside our differences, gathering together in love as brothers and sisters in the name of Christ—stepping outside of the box the world put us in by joining hearts and hands in worship and praise to the one true God—no matter what our nationality!

Over the course of our 17 years in the Philippines, our paths crossed with those from many different countries. When we returned home in 2003, we left behind precious Filipino friends whom we dearly love. We know that we could never have accomplished this miracle of unity by ourselves. It was through the power of our Lord and Savior, Jesus Christ. Through Him, we have a bond that cannot be broken. And we can declare what the Apostle Paul wrote to the Gentile believers in the book of Ephesians. We are no longer strangers and foreigners. We are citizens along with all of God's holy people. We are members of God's family. We are His house, built on the foundation of the apostles and prophets. And the cornerstone is Christ Jesus Himself. We who believe are carefully joined together (Filipino, American, German, Japanese, Canadian, Chinese, Australian), becoming a holy temple for the Lord.

March 2007

I'm scared. And I just can't seem to shake it.

Why am I so frightened? Because as I sat down on the first day of the new year to contemplate my life, I felt incredibly blessed.

I can hear the skepticism in your voice. "And feeling blessed is a good reason to be afraid?!" For me? Yes. Because I have those moments when my pessimism kicks in, and I wonder, *how long can it last?* Surely there is a catastrophic storm headed my way—a thundercloud with my name on it. Is this the calm before the raging winds blow in? Is God preparing me for a big one? I sing about raising my hands and praising the God who gives and takes away, about praising Him in the storm. Will He test me to see if I really mean what I say?

I've been walking with Christ for 30 years. You'd think that I would be breezing through life without the jaws of fear clamping down on me. I know all the right answers. I truly believe in my heart that God is good and that He causes all things to work together for good to those who love Him, to those who are called according to His purpose (see Romans 8:28). I've experienced His mercy and compassion. I'm aware of why He allows trials in my life—to help me to grow and to learn to rely on His strength. I'm convinced that His grace is sufficient for whatever comes my way. I have no doubts about His faithfulness and His promise to always be with me. I clearly understand these biblical truths. But that does not keep the apprehensions from gripping my heart. I am so fearful of losing someone I love. Because I love deeply and passionately, just the thought of having to release someone precious to me sends a chill through my heart.

I remember all too well the heartaches that followed the deaths of my grandmother when I was nine and my father when I was 17. Though long ago, the memories have never left me. I am terrified of having to relive that kind of emotional pain and grief. I've seen the way friends have been affected by death in the last few years, how their sorrow has caused intense anguish. Wives and husbands who have lost spouses. Mothers and fathers who have lost children. Grandmothers and grandfathers who have lost grandchildren. Daughters and sons who have lost parents. I know that Jesus is our comfort, and I have seen His presence be so real to these friends. But this realization does not take away their pain, nor does it seem to diminish my fear.

I ask myself: is fear the lack of faith? I remember reading somewhere that it is. But I don't think I can look at it in such black and white terms. For one thing, my experiences as a young child and a teenager are certainly legitimate causes for fear. And the personality God created me with tends to lean toward fearful emotions. I'm so thankful that my Creator remembers this as He patiently works with me. Besides, my heart tells me that if I should have to face the suffering from the death of a loved one, God will strengthen my faith when needed to enable me to endure, even in the midst of the pain.

But how do I rid myself of the horrible anticipation of that pain? I'm not sure that I will ever be completely free of it, though I want to keep on striving toward that freedom. Steve often tells me that I need to live in the moment, enjoy today. Don't worry about tomorrow and the what-ifs, because those what-ifs may never happen. "Steep your life in God-reality, God-initiative, God-provisions. Don't worry about missing out. You'll find all your everyday human concerns will be met. Give your entire attention to what God is doing right now, and don't get worked up about what may or may not happen tomorrow. God will help you deal with whatever hard things come up when the time comes" (Matthew 6:33–34, *The Message*).

I hope the fears will keep on fading as I continue to grow in intimacy with Christ. Scripture tells us that God is love and that perfect love casts out fear. These verses were the very ones that captured my heart when God was pursuing me. And they make me want to put all the more effort into drawing nearer to His heart. Jill Briscoe, in her book *Choices That Can Change a Woman's Life*, wrote, "I discovered that sorrow was not to be feared but rather endured with hope and expectancy that God would use it to visit and bless my life."

The key, I know, is taking my eyes off of myself. I must put on peripheral blinders so that my vision does not stray to the left or the right. It should not be focused on the things of this world. This can only happen as my mind is constantly being renewed through the Word of God. Then, with the help of the

Holy Spirit, I must force myself to look straight ahead into the kind and loving eyes of my Shepherd. *Turn your eyes upon Jesus, Look full in His wonderful face, And the things of earth will grow strangely dim, In the light of His glory and grace.*

April 2007

I sat in the Reagan National Airport waiting for my flight to Cleveland (via Philadelphia), which was delayed by about an hour and a half. It was difficult not to get irritated with the staff of the particular airline I was flying with. I've flown enough both domestically and internationally to know that there are circumstances beyond control, and that there are times when we have to allow for human error (in management that is, not flying!), but the lack of competent and helpful customer service was inexcusable.

Inefficiency is something I have a hard time accepting in myself, and I find that I have little patience tolerating it in others, especially when I know that they are capable of doing a better job. Impatience, I'll be the first to admit, is one of my weaknesses. It's an aspect of my personality that I don't much like. Patience is listed in the fruit of the Spirit—it's a godly virtue that should be characterized in my life. Galatians 5:22 says, "The fruit of the Spirit is love, joy, peace, patience, kindness, goodness, faithfulness, gentleness, and self-control."

Besides affecting my physical health by raising my blood pressure, getting agitated harms my spiritual and emotional well-being. So as I boarded the airplane, I had a little talk with myself. "Mary, calm down. You are not responsible for these airline agents, but you are responsible for your attitude and your response to this situation." By the time I sat down, my heart rate had slowed. I closed my eyes, taking a deep breath, as the plane took off. When we were airborne I looked out the window. The view caused my heart rate to accelerate once again, though this time with a positive exhilaration. The cityscape of Washington DC stretched below me—such an impressive sight!

Then my thoughts turned to my Virginia family. I had said goodbye to them over two hours earlier. *But,* it was not with the same sense of sadness that has accompanied so many of our previous goodbyes. This one I knew would be very temporary. In twelve days our daughter Sarah, son-in-law Brandon, and grandchildren Elena and Paul would be moving back to Northeast Ohio! YES! Can you hear the excitement in my "voice"? A new job for Brandon will bring them back to the area, as well as Sarah's desire to be close to family, and, most assuredly, the prayers of grandparents! Brandon will begin this new job in Beachwood, Ohio, on April 2, utilizing his master's degree in International Commerce.

The previous Friday I had driven back to Virginia with Sarah and the kids after their two-week visit to help pack boxes and watch my grandchildren while Sarah and Brandon sorted and packed. My daughter drove me to the airport on Tuesday, thus my experiences with—a delayed flight—and incompetent agents—and a missed flight—and large airports. Which, by the way, all suddenly seemed very unimportant. Why would I be foolish enough to allow something so insignificant to upset me and rob me of the tremendous joy of having our family living minutes away instead of hours?! Why, indeed.

May 2007

After Easter, our ABF began a series on spiritual warfare that was taught by Steve and our friends Daniel and Bruce. What a great time to study this topic, having just celebrated the victory that we have through the resurrection of our Lord and Savior, Jesus Christ!

Many in our American culture, including people in the church, do not believe in the spirit world, nor do they understand the dangers lurking around us. Philippine culture is much more aware, just as are many other Asian, African, South American, and Central American cultures. Maybe that's why Steve has been called upon several times since we returned home from the mission field to pray in situations where there was intense spiritual warfare, some of it through demonic activity. I've accompanied him on a couple of these visits. I'm sometimes nervous because of past personal experiences, but I've learned to depend upon the promise that "greater is He that is in me than he that is in the world" (see 1 John 4:4b).

About a month before the guys were to teach the spiritual warfare series, Daniel asked the class to begin praying for God's protection, for we would be walking through territory Satan wants us to be ignorant of. He prefers that we not know what he's up to. And he certainly doesn't want us to realize that we have power to fight him—the power of our risen Savior!

What does spiritual warfare look like? It can manifest itself in any and every area of our lives—spiritual, physical, emotional, and mental. Satan knows exactly where we are vulnerable, and he won't hesitate to attack us in our weakness.

We do need to be extremely careful, though, not to attribute every situation to the wiles of Satan. Remember the phrase that Flip Wilson was famous for using? —"The devil made me do it!" That can be a real cop out for not taking responsibility for our own lives. Even if Satan is to blame for much of the evil that goes on in the world, some of the situations we find ourselves in are simply due to the fact that we made wrong or foolish choices. We may be redeemed, but we are still sinners. And we live in a fallen world.

This past March, on my way back home to Ohio from Virginia, I was flying above the clouds, looking down at the earth, so high up that I couldn't see houses or cars. Only patches of land, bodies of water, and the Pennsylvania hills were visible. In my mind I visualized a battle going on—between the forces of good and the forces of evil, both armies hovering over the earth. A chill ran down my spine. That's a picture that our mortal eyes cannot see. It's another realm for sure, a spiritual one, but it is very real. Suddenly my eyes gravitated toward a spot. There, in the middle of nowhere, was a single light. I couldn't figure out what it could possibly be. I saw nothing else around it. Curious, I pointed it out to my seatmate and asked her if she knew what it was. She didn't, though she wondered if it might be a power plant. A light from a power plant piercing the darkness. How appropriate! It's only the light of the Word of God, through the power which raised Christ from the dead, that can pierce the spiritual darkness around us.

Satan knows this, and he does everything in his limited power to keep us from realizing the extent of the capabilities we have to fight and resist him. That's why it is so important for us to be in a growing, vibrant relationship with Christ. We need to be filling our minds with Scripture and praying on our knees.

R. Arthur Mathews, in his book *Born for Battle,* wrote about Satan being very much alive and ready to thwart the work that Christ did on the cross. The author also said that Satan is especially concerned about those who preach the Gospel of Christ "in earth's dark corners."

We found that last sentence true throughout our years in the Philippines. Since he couldn't have our hearts and souls, Satan cunningly set out to destroy us. He wanted to damage our testimony, to discredit the name of Jesus. The Deceiver tried to fill us with doubts and to persuade us to give up. Though there were countless incidents when the Evil One attempted to ruin us, there is one that sticks in my mind.

It was the last year of our third term. On November 20, I received a letter from my friend Sharon. This is what she wrote: "Dear Mary, I just want to write a note of encouragement to you. God is in control. What assurance we can draw from that. This past June I was listening to Chuck Swindoll's study on the life of

David. He concluded with these thoughts: 'God's solutions are strange and simple—be open; God's promotions are sudden and surprising—be ready; God's selections are sovereign and sure—be calm. We can be calm in the face of the storm. God is guiding the ship.' Mary, as you and Steve conclude these last few months, be prepared for Satan's attack. I have sensed the need to really be praying for you. I believe God has drawn a strong prayer support of people around you as you close this term in the Philippines. I do not know who any others are. I just know He has laid a heavy burden on my heart. You are being upheld."

We faced many difficult and stressful situations over that last year—some with co-workers, some with family. I often felt weary, beaten up, attacked. Steve and I talked about "putting on the full armor of God…taking up the shield of faith with which we can extinguish all the flaming arrows of the evil one" (see Ephesians 6:10-18)

Four days after I received Sharon's letter, Satan shot a flaming arrow. Hester and Micah were at school. Steve was at a meeting at Faith Academy. I was out shopping. Hot, tired, and hungry, I was looking forward to some quiet time at our apartment with a glass of cold water and a sandwich. The sight that greeted me as I turned down our street assured me that there would be no quiet retreat, but rather chaos filled with tears. Several fire trucks were parked outside our office/apartment compound. I practically flew through the gate, only to be stopped by one of our missionaries. He put his arm around me and tearfully told me what had happened. A fire had roared through our apartment. I ran up the stairs and walked into destruction.

How do you express what you are feeling when you walk into your daughter's bedroom and see her "life" in ashes? Hester was a senior in high school. When she graduated the following May, she would be leaving behind friends, school, culture that had been part of her life since she was six years old. Everything she owned that would remind her of those years was gone. Her bedroom was totally destroyed. Tears gushed from my eyes, splashing in the puddles of water at my feet. My sadness was for all that my daughter had lost. But then, I caught my breath as I realized how much more tragic this could have been. What if the fire had happened at night when Hester was asleep in her bed? It was then that I thought about the letter I read a few days earlier. Satan didn't accomplish what he set out to do, because one of the Lord's warriors was fighting for us—my dear friend at home was wrestling in prayer!

There are so many stories I could tell about how the forces of darkness were defeated in the hours and days following the fire and how God was glorified through His people. I'll leave that for another time. Instead, I close with the words of Psalm 66: "Praise our God, O peoples, let the sound of His praise be heard; He has preserved our lives and kept our feet from slipping. For You, O God, tested us; You refined us like silver. We went through fire and water, but You brought us to a place of abundance."

June 2007

After I heard the news of the tragedy that took place on the Virginia Tech campus on April 16, the first thing I wanted to do was hear my son's voice. He was living on the campus of Wheaton College in Illinois, and I needed reassurance that all was well with him. I'm sure there were other parents across the country who were experiencing the same feelings I had—an urgency to know that their sons or daughters were safe.

Twenty days after that horrible story was flashed across our television screen, I sat in the chapel on the Wheaton campus with my husband, my mother, and my daughter to witness and celebrate Micah's graduation. Joy filled our hearts to watch our youngest child walk across the stage and receive his diploma. But mixed with that, at least for me, was a sadness for those

parents who would not get the chance to honor the achieve-
ments of their sons or daughters. Instead, they are grieving the
brutal deaths of their children.

Virginia Tech was not the only college hit hard over these
last several months. Bluffton College in northwest Ohio is still
reeling from the deaths of several members of their baseball
team—not from a lone gunman, but from a serious bus accident. There was a picture in the newspaper a few weeks ago
of the parents of a young man who was injured in that same
accident. They were receiving his diploma for him since he was
not able to take part in the graduation ceremony. Many more
families should have been seated in the audience, but instead,
they may have been sitting in an empty living room or putting
flowers on a grave. It's hard to make sense of it all.

Life certainly can be puzzling at times. An *Akron Beacon
Journal* article on Virginia Tech's commencement ceremonies
that took place on May 11 and 12 stated that the school was
challenged to "strike a balance between celebration and sorrow." That's an interesting, and yet bewildering, statement. I
have struggled with this very issue over the last several months.
Striking a balance between these two emotions seems to be an
impossible task, but with the right perspective, an eternal one,
it can be accomplished.

Right here, right now, at this moment in time, my life
feels like a season of blessing. One of my favorite portions of
Scripture is Psalm 18:16–19. It says, "He reached down from
on high and took hold of me; He drew me out of deep waters.
He rescued me from my powerful enemy, from my foes who
were too strong for me. They confronted me in the day of my
disaster, *but* the Lord was my support. He brought me out into
a spacious place; He rescued me because He delighted in me"
(emphasis mine). After so many years of living overseas, of
periods of separation from loved ones, of homesickness, God
has brought me out into a spacious place.

A season of blessing—in love with Jesus. Worshiping. Reveling in His creation. Learning how much He loves me—how He delights in me!

A season of blessing—surrounded by my family. Since Micah is back home after graduation, and Sarah, Brandon, and their two children are back in Ohio and have just moved into their new house in West Akron, this is the first time in I don't know how long that we are all living in the same state for any length of time.

A season of blessing—in ministry. God has opened up so many wonderful opportunities in which to serve Him—both for Steve and for me.

A season of blessing. Unfortunately, there are also moments of temporary guilt—but only if I permit Satan to have his way. He's no dummy. Besides a few medical issues with Mom, my life is good—busy, but good. I presently have no heavy burdens to carry. However, several of my friends do. They are suffering, and that crafty serpent is aware of how that affects me. He knows where and when to attack with a guilt arrow right to my heart. Should I feel guilty? My friend Mary says I shouldn't. She reminds me that the friends who are experiencing hardship need those who are strong to pray and to help carry the burdens. There have been times in the past when in my weakness I needed someone to lift me up and to ease the weight pressing down on me. "The work is too heavy for you; you cannot handle it alone" (Exodus 18:18). I now have not only the privilege but also the responsibility to be there for my friends—listening, praying, encouraging. That puts my season of blessing, my spacious place, into a proper eternal perspective that allows me to strike a balance between celebration and sorrow.

If God delights in showering me at this time in my life, who am I to question Him or His motives? My response should be praise and thanksgiving. The Lord wants me to enjoy this season of peace and calm—accepting this season of abundance as a gift from Him—not with guilt but with a grateful heart!

Micah's college graduation

July 2007

On November 27 of last year, the Lord received one of His faithful servants and one of our dear friends into His presence. Ted's earthly journey, after a year-long battle with a cancerous brain tumor, was over. His wife, and my precious friend, Karen, carries on in the grace of God, the same grace that was manifested throughout her husband's illness. The last time Steve and I saw Ted alive, Karen commented to me that it really is true that God's grace is there just when you need it.

We visited Ted just a few short days before he was called home to glory. It pained us so to see how the disease had ravished him. He was lying in a hospital bed in the living room of their condo. A black patch covered one eye. He couldn't speak, but he could hear us. As Karen tended to something, I told Ted how much he meant to us, that we loved him, and I thanked him for all he had done for us—he was one of our biggest advocates during our time in the Philippines—Ted had a great heart for missions and a real love for missionaries.

Steve spoke to him for a few minutes, and then as he prayed, I held Ted's hand. He squeezed my hand so hard that I smiled, knowing that he was aware of our presence, and he was entering into prayer with us.

In the days following his funeral, I read the online guest book provided by the *Akron Beacon Journal*. What a testimony to the life of this beloved brother in Christ!

"Dr. Hamilton was truly a great man of integrity."

"His kind, gentle spirit will be missed by more people than you can imagine."

"We will always remember Ted's steadfast commitment to discipleship and raising up disciples who would teach others also. His legacy lives on in the many lives he influenced and the leaders who serve effectively today because of the impact Ted had on them."

"Ted was one of the kindest and most generous people I've ever met."

"Our lives in Christ today are where they are because of Ted's faithfulness to Christ."

"Dr. Hamilton was an amazing man."

"I remember him as a very gentle, funny guy who was so easy to trust and be friends with."

"Ted truly touched more lives in such a positive way that you could never comprehend the breadth."

"The world lost a great man. Ted obviously had an impact on many lives. The testimonies of so many are a living tribute to him."

"I can say the man touched my heart many, many times. He would always listen and be willing to spend time talking with each patient more like a friend."

When I spoke to Karen recently about writing this letter, she shared a few of Ted's favorite Scripture verses with me. I chose two of them that really exemplified Ted's life in my eyes—both from 2 Timothy. Chapter one, verse seven says, "For God has not given us a spirit of timidity, but of power and love and discipline." And chapter two, verse two says, "And the things which you have heard from me in the presence of many witnesses, these entrust to faithful men, who will be able to teach others also."

God was glorified in Ted's life and in his death. And He continues to receive the glory in Karen's life as the grace of the God who gives and takes away is miraculously visible, even through her sorrow and pain.

August 2007

A brilliant pink tinged the horizon—a prelude to the sun breaking forth in the eastern sky. Because my porch happens to face east, I was a spectator early one morning of this magnificent display of the Creator's handiwork. It was a quiet moment of worship—between me and my God—when I paused to allow the Spirit to fill me with His peace. I felt bathed in His love.

I've needed that reassurance of His love—to have His mercy fall fresh on me—as I have journeyed into my past in an attempt to write my story. The seeds for this effort began with the urgings of a friend to share with other women what God has done in my life. Those seeds then took root during a Beth Moore conference simulcast that I attended in Sugar Creek, Ohio. Beth was sharing from 2 Corinthians 3:12–18: "Therefore, since we have such a hope, we are very bold. We are not like Moses, who would put a veil over his face to keep the Israelites from gazing at it while the radiance was fading away. But their minds were made dull, for to this day the same veil remains when the old covenant is read. It has not been removed, because only in Christ is it taken away. Even to this day when Moses is read, a veil covers their hearts. *But whenever anyone turns to the Lord, the veil is taken away.* Now the Lord is the Spirit, and *where the Spirit is there is freedom.* And we, *who with unveiled faces all reflect the Lord's glory*, are being transformed into His likeness with ever-increasing glory, which comes from the Lord who is the Spirit" (emphasis mine). Beth talked about removing the veil from our hearts, making ourselves vulnerable, and openly sharing with others what amazing things God has done in our lives. This should not only draw people to the Lord, but also bring a sense of freedom to our own hearts. I came away from the conference wondering if maybe God was speaking to me. I tucked that thought away in my mind.

Though the seeds took root that day, they didn't start to germinate until several weeks later. The thought that I had tucked away just kept pushing through the soil of my mind. It was stubborn, persistent, and refused to be ignored. Finally, I prayed and sought counsel from my husband. He encouraged me to write my story.

It was an emotional and difficult journey as I had to re-live some painful episodes in my life. I was forced to walk through the darkness that had descended on me, not once, but several times, to walk through the depression that had engulfed me. I was compelled to explore a mosaic of memories, to analyze terrifying nightmares, to examine paralyzing fears, to probe the reasons for anger. The whole experience drained me. It consumed me to the point that I had to walk away from it for several days.

While on this self-imposed short "sabbatical," I found this quote by Oswald Chambers in *My Utmost for His Highest*. He writes, "The great mystical work of the Holy Spirit is in the dim regions of our personality which we cannot get at. Read the 139th Psalm; the psalmist implies, 'Thou art the God of the early mornings, the God of the late at nights, the God of the mountain peaks, and the God of the sea; but, my God, my soul has further horizons than the early mornings, deeper darkness than the nights of earth, higher peaks than any mountain peaks, greater depths than any sea in nature—Thou who art the God of all these, be my God. I cannot reach to the heights or to the depths; there are motives I cannot trace, dreams I cannot get at—my God, search me out.'"

The Holy Spirit was doing His great, mystical work in the dim regions of my personality that I was not able to get at without His help. "My God, search me out!"

When I sat down at my computer again, I knew that God understood my pain, and He was walking with me through it. I felt His holy hands on my shoulders, comforting me with His love and peace. I became aware of an overwhelming sense of grace flooding my soul. As I typed the last word, I knew what Beth said, what 2 Corinthians 3:17 said, was true. "Where the Spirit of the Lord is, there is freedom."

I finished writing my story. My desire now is that my unveiled heart will reflect the Lord's glory, because when all is said and done, it's not really my story at all—it's *His* story—the story of His redeeming love!

September 2007

Traffic was crazy as always. Slow-moving. Bumper-to-bumper. The temperature outside was probably about 31 degrees Celsius, which is approximately 89 degrees Fahrenheit, though it felt much hotter due to the high humidity. I was thankful for the car air-conditioner. At least my skin was cool inside our white Toyota. That's more than I could say for my temper as my car crawled along the congested streets. Just a typical day in Metro Manila!

The thoughts of a cold glass of water and a sandwich, accompanied with peace and quiet, made me anxious to get back to our apartment. My energy was depleted after what should have been a quick trip—*if* I had been running errands in Akron, Ohio! It seemed that things always took three times as long in this large, third-world city of Manila. I have to chuckle when people here in our average-size U.S. city complain about traffic jams.

The scene that greeted me as I turned down our street dashed all my hopes of a quiet afternoon. Several fire trucks were parked outside our mission office/apartment compound, blocking my way. I jumped from my car in a panic and practically flew through the gate, only to be stopped by one of our missionaries. He tearfully told me that a fire had roared through our apartment. I ran up the steps and walked into destruction. Chaos. Smoke. Firemen milling about. Broken glass. Water flooding the floor. Ruined furniture. Hester's bedroom totally destroyed.

God be praised that no one had been at home. My husband Steve, daughter Hester, and son Micah, were all at Faith Academy—the kids in classes and Steve at a board meeting. I suddenly was grateful for the crazy traffic that had prevented me from getting home sooner.

Discombobulated. Is that even a word? It was how I felt. I just walked around the apartment as if in a daze. What should I do? Should I start cleaning up? What should I do? Then I heard my husband's voice calling out my name. As I turned, we looked into each others' eyes, and he wrapped his strong arms around me. This was my safe place. It wasn't until I was in Steve's arms that I allowed my tears to fall. Soon sobs were shaking my body.

The storm inside me gradually calmed. Steve told me that after he was called out of the meeting, he took Hester and Micah out of class to tell them what had happened and to pray with them. They would be home at the normal time, after school let out for the day. It was then that I had the overwhelming need to talk to my daughters Sarah and Ruthanne. Both of our daughters were living in Akron with my best friend Joan and attending Malone College. I desperately wanted to hear their voices—my mother's heart craved that connection. I went into the office to make the international call. Unfortunately, neither one of them were at home. I spoke to my friend for a few minutes and then wandered back into the apartment. Steve walked with me into Hester's bedroom. I can't even begin to describe how I felt. Hester was a senior in high school. When she graduated the following May, she would be leaving behind friends, school, culture that had been part of her life since she was six years old. Except for fifth grade and ninth grade in the States, she had attended Faith Academy every year since second grade. Of all our children, she had adjusted best to Philippine culture. She spoke fluent Tagalog. I have a picture of her in a bicycle sidecar when she was six years old—the only blonde amongst the dark-haired Filipino children. Everything she owned that would remind her of her wonderful years in the Philippines was gone, lying in ashes. My heart was breaking for my daughter. My sadness was for all that she had lost. But then I caught my breath as I realized how much more tragic this could have been. What if the fire had happened at night when Hester was asleep in her bed?

As I peered into her closet that was now empty, all of her clothes having been burned up in the fire, I remembered that Hester and I had gone shopping the day before, looking for a dress for her to wear to the upcoming Christmas banquet. She found one that looked darling on her. And it, too, was gone. I began to weep again, my tears splashing in the puddles of water at my feet.

School was finally out for the day, and the Faith Academy van pulled up in front of our apartment. Steve and I went downstairs to meet the kids. When I saw my daughter, I couldn't hold back the tears. I hugged her and said, "Oh, Hester, your banquet dress." She pulled back from me a bit and replied, "No, Mom, it's okay. I took my dress to school today to show my friends."

Ohhhhh. A small thing, for sure, but in the midst of this devastation, it felt like a tremendous blessing. We walked back upstairs with the kids and into the apartment. They wandered through the rooms—Micah's room had a lot of damage, but it was Hester's room where the fire had started. There was nothing left but her charred bed and piles of ashes. I watched my daughter closely. Tears filled her eyes. For a brief moment, I thought I saw a sorrow flash across her face, but then she calmly said, "It's just stuff." She must have had the same realization I had had earlier—she could have been asleep in her bed! Her perspective and attitude toward this calamity were positive. She reminded us all that God was in control. I was so proud of her response.

We started to gather up whatever clothes we could find and any other salvageable belongings to take with us to our mission guest house. The small apartment in the guest house was completely furnished, so we didn't need to worry about dishes or sheets or towels. But something inside of me went into survival mode. I randomly grabbed pictures, knick knacks, anything that I could get my hands on that would connect me to my home. We packed up our car and traveled the short distance to the guest house. I carefully placed the objects I brought around the living room. For some odd reason, it made me feel better to see these things in the place that would be home for the remainder of our third term. I guess it was a "woman thing"—a nesting instinct—the need to make a home for my family.

Later that night, after Hester and Micah were asleep, Steve and I finally fell into bed. I lay there for awhile, listening to the noises outside. A sudden urge made me get out of bed—I needed to make sure my children were safe. I tiptoed into the other bedroom and stood there for the longest time, staring at my daughter and my son. Tears trickled down my cheeks. I whispered a prayer of thanks and then went back to my bed where I fell asleep nuzzled up against my husband.

Hester's bedroom

October 2007

The "church" is not a magnificent cathedral in Europe. Or a covered basketball court in the Philippines. Or benches under a tree in Africa. It's not an air-conditioned building with padded pews in the U.S. The church is a living entity. It's the Body of Christ. It's people. Regardless of what country you live in. Or what language you speak. It's people ministering together—offering cups of cold water to a desperate and dying world in the name of Jesus. It's people ministering to each other—loving one another—caring for one another—building one another up—helping to carry one another's burdens.

What might that look like in the life of an American missionary living in the Philippines? Just the term "American" conjures up images of wealth to most Filipinos. Though we lived comfortably enough, we were far from rich according to American standards. We always had a roof over our heads, though. And we never wondered where our next meal was going to come from. Our children went to a missionary kids' school where they received an excellent education. We had many advantages over the people we worked with. The love of Christ compelled us to share our "wealth" with both our brothers and sisters in Christ *and* with those outside the "walls" of the church. Can you imagine looking into the eyes of a hungry child? It was heart-wrenching! How could we not help in some way? We usually did not give money, having been warned by our Christian friends that syndicates preyed on children (and adults), teaching them how to look sad and pitiful so that someone would feel sorry for them and hand over a few pesos. For this reason, we kept small bags of uncooked rice or crackers in the car to give to those begging on the streets. Opportunities arose within the church as well—helping with children's education, providing food, sharing resources.

We know what it's like to be on the receiving end. There were many occasions when Steve was in school that we were in need and had to ask for help. And then, of course, as missionaries preparing to go to the field, we had to raise support. It puts you in a very humbling position. So it felt good to be on the giving end when we lived in the Philippines.

Was this a one-sided endeavor within the church? Was the missionary the one who was always giving? Absolutely not! Filipinos are such a hospitable people, always willing to share what they have. And some have very little. We were careful not to visit someone during mealtime, or we might be offered food that was intended for another family member. But usually what we received was not tangible—it was far more precious—friendship, cultural insight, spiritual fellowship.

On the day of the fire in our apartment, and for several days afterwards, we found ourselves once again on the receiving end. The Body of Christ came together and ministered to us in such a tremendous way that the memory is still fresh in my mind. Besides our mission leadership, our Filipino friends were some of the first to arrive at our apartment.

Thankfully, an older Filipino who was doing some work in the office was there when the fire trucks finally made an appearance. The firemen vacillated, most likely waiting for a bribe, typically commenting that there was no water. When they realized that they would not be getting any extra pesos, they "miraculously" found that there indeed was water. Once the fire was out, they started walking through the apartment looking for items that they could help themselves to. The Filipino worker followed the firemen around. They told him to leave, but he very firmly said he was in charge. His presence prevented them from ransacking our apartment.

My friends Menchie and Mags sifted through the ashes in Hester's bedroom, looking for anything that might be salvageable. Others came and swept water out of the apartment. Some brought food. My friend Ana ran out to the market and bought underwear for Hester. These dear friends helped in any way they could. They prayed with us, cried with us. The Body of Christ in action.

Our mission organization, both on the field and in the Michigan-based home office, was a great encouragement to us. They stood with us, and we so appreciated their support during this difficult time. It especially blessed my heart to see the little girls, daughters of our missionaries, filled with compassion for Hester. They just couldn't imagine their bedrooms and clothes and treasures being burned up in a fire. These sweet girls emptied their piggy banks, and even parted with favorite stuffed animals. The Body of Christ in action.

Bob, the missions' pastor at our home church in Akron, made an international call to our guest house the evening of the fire. Just hearing his voice brought a measure of comfort to our hearts. His care and concern, accompanied with the offer of financial assistance, meant so much to us. The Body of Christ in action.

The love shown to Hester at Faith Academy was unbelievable. I still get emotional thinking about it. The day after the fire, the principal called Hester out of chapel. She was president of her senior class, and he cooked up some excuse to get her out of the room. The story of the fire was told, and a collection was taken. The students, teachers, and faculty dug deep into their pockets. Many wrote notes of comfort and encouragement. Some of her friends brought in clothes to share. The Body of Christ in action.

Friends at home prayed. They sent monetary gifts so we could buy clothes. We were overwhelmed with their generosity. Some even requested that Hester use the money to replace items that would years later remind her of the time she lived in the Philippines. The Body of Christ in action.

I recently told parts of this story to some friends over breakfast one morning. We were sitting around the table of our friends Mary and Karl. Mary's Aunt Ruth was visiting from

Florida. She lost her home and everything she had in a tropical storm—Hurricane Charlie. This godly woman looked at me with tears in her eyes and said, "Didn't you have to pray and ask for receiving grace?" Receiving grace. I like that. It's true that it's wonderful to be able to give—it makes us feel good. But it can be very hard to receive—it sometimes makes us feel embarrassed or inadequate. Our pride can get in the way—either we won't ask for help, or we reject it when it's offered. God not only wants us to be cheerful givers, but also He wants us to be gracious receivers.

Refusing help from our brothers and sisters after the fire would have been like a slap in the face. We would have denied them the blessing that came from sharing the love of Christ with us. Was it humbling? Yes. But it was not a negative emotion, because God gave receiving grace.

What Satan initially intended for harm and destruction, God used for good. His people rose to the challenge and won the battle. They were victorious because they responded with Christ's love. And oh how we felt loved! Cared for. Built up. Strengthened to carry on.

No, the church is not a building. It's a living, breathing......
FAMILY!

November 2007

Marriage is a mystery. Two hearts joined together—spiritually, emotionally, physically. No longer two, but one. The two become one flesh.

Marriage is a picture of Christ and the Church. Ephesians 5:32 calls this a "profound mystery." It takes some radical thinking to process what this truly means. The Apostle Paul wrote in this same chapter, "Wives, submit to your husbands as to the Lord. For the husband is the head of the wife as Christ is the head of the Church, His body, of which He is the Savior. Now as the Church submits to Christ, so also wives should submit to their husbands in everything. Husbands, love your wives just as Christ loved the Church and gave Himself up for her to make her holy, cleansing her by the washing with water through the word, and to present her to Himself as a radiant church, without stain or wrinkle or any other blemish, but holy and blameless. In this same way, husbands ought to love their wives as their own bodies. He who loves his wife loves himself. After all, no one ever hated his own body, but he feeds and cares for it, just as Christ does the Church—for we are members of His body. 'For this reason a man will leave his father and mother and be united to his wife, and the two will become one flesh.' This is a profound mystery—but I am talking about Christ and the Church. However, each one of you also must love his wife as he loves himself, and the wife must respect her husband."

Not long ago, at a Sunday evening "Illuminate" service, Pastor Paul preached on the above verses. He spoke about husbands loving their wives just as Christ loved the church. I wonder if I have ever really comprehended what that love involves. Pastor Paul gave three key points that I jotted down in my Bible. Number one: it's a love that saves, that rescues. Number two: it nurtures, cares for and feeds. Number three: it loves with a mysterious love.

Steve and I celebrated our 35th wedding anniversary on September 9. As I traveled those 35 years in my memory, the Lord brought Pastor Paul's message to my mind, and I realized that this is just what my husband has been doing—loving me as Christ loves the church—with a mysterious love, a love that covers a multitude of sins, an unconditional love. Yes, it's still a human love, from one whose attempt, much to his dismay, sometimes falls short of Christ's example. But I know Steve's heart. He desires to love as Christ loves.

Having recently spent time analyzing my life, which was a pre-requisite to writing my story, I became aware of the fact that there were many instances in my past when I expected Steve to be my Savior. This was not only unhealthy, but unrealistic as well. Even after I became a Christian, there were times that I wondered if maybe I relied too much on my husband, put too much responsibility on his shoulders. As my relationship with the Lord has grown, though, along with my understanding of His Word, I've come to the conclusion that I'm not too far off the mark. No, Steve could not be, nor never can be, my Savior (with a capital S). That's Jesus' responsibility. But he has been given the command to love me with a love that saves (with a small s). With a love that rescues, that protects, that nurtures.

On the day of our anniversary, Steve had the privilege of not only baptizing our godson Dan and his wife, Stacy, but also helping them to renew their wedding vows. He asked Dan these questions: "Will you love Stacy as Christ loves the Church, being filled with the Spirit of God's power and love? Will you demonstrate that agape love in a willingness to sacrifice on her behalf? Will you live in an understanding way with your wife, never using coercive power, but love, as your motivation? Will you pray for her regularly, especially when you cannot reach agreement on important issues? Will you, with God's strength, help Stacy to grow in the grace and knowledge of the Lord Jesus Christ and help her follow Christ in all the will of God? Do you agree to exercise your God-given role as spiritual leader in the home so that she might become all that God has designed and gifted her to be in Christ?"

That's heavy-duty stuff! The Lord will hold husbands accountable for the way they treat their wives. They will have to answer to Him if they fail in this most important calling. That means no abuse of any kind—physical, sexual, mental, emotional, verbal. When Steve succeeds at loving me as Christ loves the Church, I want to respond to him with love and submission and respect. He enables me to fulfill my calling as his wife. And as a result, I find security in his love. I think that's why, at times, I become frightened at the thought of losing him. As a believer in Jesus Christ, I know that ultimately my security is in Him. But I can't shy away from the fact that He was the One who gave this man to me. He was the One who instituted marriage when He brought Adam and Eve together. My life is intertwined with Steve's. We are one flesh. That is the mystery. And that is why if he were taken away from me for some reason, I would feel like half a person. I know that doesn't sound very spiritual, but it's reality.

As the first anniversary of our friend Ted's home going approaches this month, I can't help but remember something that his wife, Karen, said not long ago. "I don't know who I'm supposed to be without Ted." Whether a husband is absent because of death or through the pain of divorce, wives have told me that they feel lost, disconnected, fragmented. God, through His grace, can bring healing and wholeness again. Time heals all wounds, they say. For some, that can be a very long time. My friend, Marie Netti, says it well. She is still in the seemingly endless process of recovering and healing from a painful divorce. With her permission I share this poem she wrote:

Caterpillar Dreams

What does a caterpillar dream in its cocoon
Where changes come slowly, like a rug on a loom
Does she wait in hope of better things
Of spacious places and flight on wings
Does she even know what she will be
Or does she feel lost
Like a boat without oars on the sea

As she waits time carves out patience with slow
*   moving hands*

*And change brings fear and wondering to unknown
  circumstance*
But loving trust in her Creator is guardian of her peace
For He knows the way He made her
And her purposes He will keep

*His faithfulness becomes a light when darkness is
  all around*
His loving presence company when loneliness abounds
*In the quiet stillness He watches, keeping her safe
  from harm*
And comfort to her soul is found in leaning on His arm

One day the darkness will be shed for the light
Once stilled movements will come with ease
There'll be no trace of the old ways in sight
And in freedom she'll rise on the breeze

But for now she waits with patience
Though long the time may seem
As God makes her a new creation
In the days of caterpillar dreams

December 2007

"How can I say thanks for the things You have done for me?
Things so undeserved, yet You give to prove Your love for me.
The voices of a million angels could not express my gratitude.
All that I am and ever hope to be, I owe it all to Thee. To God
be the glory. To God be the glory. To God be the glory for the
things He has done." (Andrae Crouch)

We gather together with family and friends on a Thursday
in November every year to give thanks, hopefully to the One
who is worthy of our thanks—the Giver of Life. I fear that

Thanksgiving in this country has succumbed to secular influence, just as Christmas and Easter have. Our society is reaping the consequences of taking God out of not just these "holy" days, but also removing Him from our daily lives.

That's why, as a follower of Jesus Christ, I must make the effort each day to give glory where glory is due. Otherwise, the world's values will gradually result in an ungrateful heart. I don't want that. So I will continue to thank God for His blessings, His gifts of love, His guidance, His grace in the tough times, His provision over the years.

I love when our family gets together and reminisces about the past—laughing at the humorous things we've done or said, remembering people who have crossed our paths, thinking back at the ways God has worked in our lives and how He has miraculously provided for us....

The money sat on the dresser in our bedroom in the little apartment in Cicero, Illinois, on the outskirts of Chicago. I walked by that dresser several times over a two-day period, looking at the money. My hand even reached out a few times to grab the 50 dollar bill into my fist, but I resisted. My stomach growled. Our refrigerator was empty. There was no milk to give our three daughters. No food except for corn meal mush. No butter or syrup to make the mush more appealing to taste. Surely God wouldn't mind that a mother take that money and buy food for her hungry children. But that money had been promised for someone else.

Two days earlier my husband Steve had preached at a Filipino American church in Chicago. On the drive to the church on that Sunday Steve told me that if he were given an honorarium for speaking he would give it to Matt and Penny. This young couple was being sent out by the church we attended to plant a church in rural

Illinois. So the money sat, and I grew a little angrier with each passing hour. We went to bed Tuesday night knowing what it was like to wonder where our next meal would come from. Leftover mush on Wednesday. That evening I readied myself for prayer meeting and AWANA. Steve was not able to be there as he had a big project due for a class at Moody Bible Institute. He handed me the money and asked me to pass it on to Matt and Penny with our prayers. I did so, a bit grudgingly. Then I went to take care of my duties as AWANA secretary.

Not even ten minutes had passed when someone walked up to me and handed me an envelope. Inside was a monetary gift—two times the amount that we had given to Matt and Penny! I was stunned! Tears were running down my face as I called Steve with the news. He didn't seem surprised. His faith was such that he knew without a doubt that God would provide for our needs. The evening was still young, and God wasn't finished showing me His miracles.

I went to choir practice after AWANA. As I walked down the aisle afterwards, headed for the door, a middle-aged man stopped me. Ray asked where my car was parked. I pointed to the side parking lot, and he said he would meet me there. Ray and Inga proceeded to empty their trunk and fill my trunk with bag after bag of groceries. I hugged this generous couple as I tearfully thanked them. Neither Ray and Inga nor our other friend had an inkling of what we as a family had just gone through. But our great God knew. He provided above and beyond what we had given to Matt and Penny. My humble heart acknowledged my lack of faith. I had to confess my earlier attitude of resentment and thank Him for His generosity and for His willingness to honor even my reluctant obedience.

It's my belief that God understood the struggle going on inside of me as a mother watching my children go to bed hungry. He didn't delight in our plight, but He knew it was a necessary lesson in His faithfulness for that moment in my life. He has used it in countless ways over the years to remind me of His trustworthiness. At that time I had no idea whatsoever that some day we would be missionaries in the Philippines, surrounded by people who would live day to day wondering where their next meal would come from.

Five years later, after many more lessons, that's just what we were—missionaries in the Philippines. Before we could share the Bread of Life with Filipinos, satisfying their spiritual hunger, we needed to give physical nourishment. And it was helpful that we knew what it felt like to be hungry. Though we only experienced that in a small way and for a short time several years before, we still remembered that gnawing in the pit of our stomachs.

Every time God allows us to care for someone's basic needs, whether in the Philippines or here in Ohio, I think of the many ways He has provided and the many people He has used in our lives. The above story was just one of many stories—it wasn't an isolated moment in time, a rare occurrence—it was a chapter in the continuing saga of the Bucys, revealing the continuing faithfulness of our God, who is worthy of our thanks, not just on Turkey Day but all year long.

January 2008 #1

Words. Not directed at me personally, and I'm sure their intent was not necessarily to cause pain. Yet I took them personally because of the circumstances of which they spoke. And they did indeed hurt.

I sat on the chair in our ABF for several minutes, my mind filled with those words. The longer I allowed the words to stay there, the more my attitude was affected. I didn't like how I was feeling. In less than thirty minutes we would be leaving the classroom and going into the sanctuary for the worship service. Could I really worship the Lord when my heart was struggling so? I stood up and walked out into the atrium where I found a table off in a corner. I asked the Lord to please deal with my attitude, and to help me sort through my hurt feelings. Looking out the window, it was almost as if I heard a gentle whisper. I opened my Bible to Psalm 51. Yes, there it was. Verse 10. "Create in me a pure heart, O God, and renew a steadfast spirit within me." I went back to verse one to read through the whole psalm and then turned the pages to Philippians 4:8–9. "Finally, brothers [and sisters], whatever is true, whatever is noble, whatever is right, whatever is pure, whatever is lovely, whatever is admirable—if anything is excellent or praise-worthy—think about such things. Whatever you have learned or received or heard from me, or seen in me—put it into practice. And the God of peace will be with you."

I closed my Bible, glanced across the room, and saw a friend whom I greatly admire—a safe friend – a godly and wise woman. I know her well. She prays for me daily. And I knew that she would listen carefully and that she would pray for the Lord to work in me. We sat down together, and she let me share, without judging me.

My heart was ready for worship. It was beautiful, and the message was wonderful. Pastor Paul took us back to the beginning, before Christmas, even before creation—speaking of the eternal existence of the Son of God.

After lunch, I laid down on the couch in our living room and took a two-hour nap. I never sleep that long on Sunday afternoons. Normally I just doze in my recliner. But I was emotionally exhausted. Later in the day my husband Steve and I talked through what had happened that morning. As always, he guided me to the right perspective. I remembered that love covers a multitude of sins—and hurts—and offenses. There are times when I really need to examine the reason behind someone's words. Maybe that person is hurting and struggling with some hard issues. Maybe he or she is going through a difficult season of life. These are times when I need to overlook the things that come out of people's mouths. However, that's not always the case. There are offenses that God would have us confront and deal with in order that a relationship not be severed. After much thought, I realized that this was not one of those times when confrontation would be helpful.

When I woke up on Monday morning, the feelings tried to rear their ugly heads again. I really didn't want to go there, so I vehemently refused to give myself (and Satan) the green light to disrupt my day. That afternoon my friend called. She had prayed for me that morning—probably right around the time I was battling my thoughts. Thank You, Lord, for faithful friends! She said something that made me stop and think. It was her opinion, and she felt strongly about it, that Satan was trying his hardest to distract me from what God wants me to do. The Lord has opened up an opportunity for me to share my story at a women's conference at The Chapel in February. I think she may be on to something. I guess our Women's Ministry team knew what they were talking about when they advised us to have our prayer partners praying *now* for the conference that is still more than a month away. It's a given that the enemy will be working against us. The last thing he wants is for us to tell about the victories we have received in and through Jesus Christ.

A few evenings later, I felt a knot in the middle of my shoulders—a sure sign of stress. A good night's sleep would work wonders. The next morning my jaw hurt. I tend to grind my teeth when I'm concentrating or stressed about something. Well this must have meant that I hadn't totally let go of my feelings. It was something I desperately needed to do.

I wrapped myself in an afghan, fixed a cup of hot chocolate, and sat on my new back porch that was enclosed with new windows this past summer. A holly bush sat on the small outside porch. It was quiet and peaceful. The music from a Hillsong Ultimate Worship CD played in the kitchen and floated out onto the porch:

> *Find rest my soul*
> *In Christ alone.*
> *Know His power*
> *In quietness and trust.*

I stared out the window at my backyard that was covered with newly fallen snow, pristine white, without blemish. My thoughts drifted back to Psalm 51, specifically verses 7–8: "Cleanse me with hyssop, and I will be clean; wash me, and I will be whiter than snow. Let me hear joy and gladness." I asked God to please wash me white as the snow that blanketed my yard. My eye caught a flash of red as a cardinal flew into the tree tops. Smaller birds flitted from one bird feeder to another. My ears heard their songs of joy. And I found rest for my soul. In quietness and trust—in Christ alone.

January 2008 #2

New Year's Day. A time that I looked back over the previous year. Reflecting. Remembering. Analyzing. 2007—an amazing year for me. The Lord brought a freedom into my life like none I've ever experienced before. However, it required that I travel down the long corridor of yesteryears.

The hallway was lined with doors on each side, some open, some closed. The first part of my journey was a pleasant stroll down memory lane, stopping to gaze at the portraits on the walls of people who had been part of my life. Now and then I would happen upon a door that stood wide open. If the room held good memories, I'd run inside, sit down in a rocking chair, and let my mind wander through those happy times. If the room held bad memories, I'd tip-toe in, look around, breathe a sigh of relief, and whisper a prayer of thanksgiving that God had seen me through those difficult times. The windows were open in all of these rooms, allowing the sun to shine through and the curtains to flutter in the fresh breeze.

When I approached a closed door, I usually hesitated before I turned the doorknob. Then I'd slowly push the door open, peeking inside with trepidation filling my heart. As I walked into the room, I asked the Lord for grace to face whatever I'd see. After re-living the memories, I'd unclench my tightly closed fists, skip over to the window, throw it open, and willingly send those memories to Jesus. The gentle wind blowing through my hair smelled clean and sweet.

I continued my pilgrimage, enjoying the open doors and finding victory as I walked through the closed doors. But down at the end of the hallway was one door that I could not open. No matter how hard I pushed, it would not budge. It was locked. I looked back down the hall. All the doors were now open. All but this one. I panicked a bit, realizing that I could not finish my journey without knowing what lay behind that door. Trying not to hyperventilate, I whispered my Savior's name—"Jesus." And there He was, standing by my side. The Keeper of the keys. As He put the key in the lock, I started trembling. I yelled, "STOP!" But He laid His hand on my shoulder, reassuring me, and continued to unlock the door. He pushed it open. I just stood there, not able to move. "Go in," He encouraged. I closed my eyes tightly and shuffled into the room. A foul odor permeated the air. My stomach roiled, nauseating me to the point that I thought I would vomit. The heckling voice of the enemy of my soul bounced off the walls. I was shaking with fear and felt so alone. But then I heard Jesus say, "Open your eyes. I am right here with you." I did as He told me to do, but I couldn't see anything clearly through the haze. Then as my eyes focused, I could see that the room was heavily polluted—with guilt and shame. *My* guilt. And *my* shame. The pain piercing my heart caused me to fall to the filthy floor. With my forehead pressed against the grime, the sound of sobbing reverberated through the room. It took me a few minutes before I recognized that the sound was coming from my own mouth, wrenched from the deepest parts of my being.

And then I felt myself being tenderly lifted up into the strong arms of my Shepherd. He held me close to His heart and whispered into my ear. "Shhh. Don't cry, little lamb. It's okay. You have carried the burden of your guilt and shame much too long. That really wasn't necessary, you know, because I had already taken care of them. When you came to My cross back in 1976, I didn't just offer you forgiveness, taking your sins away. I also took your guilt and shame. But you held on to them. Please give them to Me now, Mary. They are no longer yours to carry." I looked up into the kind eyes of Jesus. What I saw in those eyes caused me to gasp in delight—such love and compassion! My tears of sorrow instantly turned into tears of joy. He set my feet upon the floor. I walked over to the window, with Him never leaving my side. And together we threw open the window. The sunshine felt warm on my face. The room was filled with a brilliant light, for the wind had blown all traces of the pollution away. The sickening smell and the taunting noises that greeted me when I first entered the room were gone, banished by the Word of God. They were replaced with a pleasing aroma and the musical laughter of Jesus. The breeze of the Holy Spirit swept through my soul, clearing it of all the junk that had littered it for so long. My spirit soared! With my arms stretched out, I twirled round and round, giggling like a little girl. I was FREE!

New Year's Day. A time when I looked ahead to the coming year. Anticipating. Wondering what the days and months will hold for me. 2008. I entered through this new door—in freedom—trusting the good, faithful, and holy One, who holds my future in His nail-scarred hands.

February 2008

A sadness filled my heart when a North American missionary woman made the statement that we could never really be close to Filipinas because of cultural differences. How thankful I am that she was wrong! I have a picture sitting on the desk in my living room of me with five of my special Filipina friends. My conclusion? *Culture* does not matter when the hearts of women are connected.

I'm part of a prayer circle for a missionary friend. She calls us her "142:7 Women" taken from Psalm 142, verse 7. "Your people will form a *circle* around me and You'll bring me showers of blessing!" This friend lives 10,000 miles away in the Philippines. My conclusion? *Distance* does not matter when the hearts of women are connected.

I sat in a Mexican restaurant observing my two friends—one with dark skin and black hair, the other with light skin and blonde hair. They care deeply about each other. These women are my sisters in Christ, and I love them both dearly.

My conclusion? *Color* does not matter when the hearts of women are connected.

We get together at Christmas time for breakfast, and periodically during the year. These friends went to grade school with me 40 plus years ago! My conclusion? *Time* does not matter when the hearts of women are connected.

A dear friend is 19 years older than I am. Another is 28 years younger than I am—the same age as one of my daughters! My conclusion? *Age* does not matter when the hearts of women are connected.

Another missionary friend asked me to be part of her prayer circle. She lives in the Middle East and often talks about her Muslim friends. My conclusion? *Religion* does not matter when the hearts of women are connected.

My favorite book/movie is *Anne of Green Gables*. In the book, Anne refers to Diana as her "bosom friend" and her "kindred spirit." How many of us long for that kind of relationship, for a soul sister who touches our hearts? For a friendship that allows us to be different and still accept one another? One that gives us the power to extend the same kind of grace that has been extended to us, and the ability to love each other with a love that never fails?

Women were created for relationship. As I think back over the years, the faces of the many women who have wandered into my life fill my mind. Some wandered back out, for various reasons. Our hearts connected for a moment in time, filling a particular need at a particular season in our lives. They may no longer be part of my world, but their memory remains a cherished part of my past. And then there are those that stayed. Steadfast. Immovable. Enduring, loving, and praying. Women who have stood the test of time.

I recently read this statement: "Prayer is holding a person's name in your heart." Isn't that beautiful? Whether you are my mother, my daughter, my sister-in-law, my cousin, my friend—if you live in another state or another country—if I see you frequently, occasionally, or haven't seen you in years—if I know you well or haven't really had the opportunity yet—I feel a connection to you as I share my deepest thoughts and emotions, my very heart with you. Please know that I hold your name in my heart. What better time to remind you than during the month we celebrate Valentine's Day, the season of hearts! And to let you know that when I send my letters, either through e-mail or by putting a label on an envelope, I always lift you up by name to the Throne of Grace—to the God who knows you by name, to the Savior who has carved you on the palms of His hands, to the Shepherd who carries you close to His heart. To Jesus who loves you with an everlasting love.

March 2008

Reading is like breathing for me. I always have a stack of books sitting next to my recliner or in the nightstand next to my bed. Books are my friends and have been for most of my life, both in healthy ways and unhealthy ways.

I was so excited when I first learned to read, when all those letters printed on a page finally started to make sense. My first library card was a cherished possession. The library gave me access to shelves upon shelves of books that opened up new worlds for me. In the evenings, after supper, when the street lights came on, playtime was over and all the neighborhood kids went to their homes, I snuggled up on a chair in the living room with a book. Since I had no siblings to play with, I entertained myself with books. They were my companions. Even at a young age I was capable of entering into the stories I read. I wasn't shy, bashful little Mary—instead I was the main character of the book.

I remember going to the store (Kresges or Woolworths or Spartans) with my cousin Sally to look for Nancy Drew books. If

I remember correctly, she'd buy one and I'd buy a different one so we could trade. Oh the adventures I had with Nancy Drew!

During my early adolescence, still being a very shy young girl, I gravitated to books about girls who were outgoing and pretty and popular—everything that I believed I wasn't—contributing to the make-believe world that I often lived in.

In my later teen years, after my dad had died, books filled the sometimes lonely moments of my life. My boyfriend had left for the night. My girlfriends were all at their homes. My mom was out. It was just me and my books. Or occasionally a different form of storytelling—the television set. Watching TV didn't require as much imagination as reading a book, but it still allowed me to escape into fantasy.

Eventually adventure and high school popularity books gave way to romance stories. I suppose most of them were in-nocent enough—the kind with the dashing hero or the knight in shining armor. When I was twenty-one I married my dashing hero. We were very much in love. But I soon discovered that real life did not play out like the romance novels. The armor on my knight was not always shining and even had some dents in it. Steve found out that his bride was at times a demanding, spoiled brat. I realized that there were occasions when my hero was not able to rescue me. I learned that childbirth was painful, and cute little babies kept you up at night. My life was not going to be the perfect life that I'd read about for so many years. You'd think this realization would have caused me to pitch those books out the window. But it had the opposite affect. I read more.

Then our lives were turned upside down and inside out by Jesus Christ. Suddenly I had *the* Book in my hands, reading the greatest story ever told, about the Master Storyteller Himself! My love affair with books continued, but now I was reading Christian novels and books that would help me to grow spiritu-ally. It was in the Bible and other Christian books that I found my true Hero.

Several years later, when I was going through an extremely difficult period of my life as a first-term missionary in the Philippines, books became a means of running away. I was desperate to remove myself from the situation I was in, so I read anything and everything I could get my hands on. Reverting back to my old habits with books and living in a make-believe world eventually caused me to slide into a pit of depression that I could not drag myself out of. I was a damsel in distress. My Immortal Hero had to rescue me. And my mortal hero helped Him. Talk about a love story!

I still enjoy reading; in fact, I devour books. But I don't have the need any longer to lose myself in a book. I want to live *my* story, not someone else's. My life, my book is still being written. I don't know what the remaining chapter titles will be. However, I do know what the ending will be—"*The princess lived happily ever after with her Prince!*"

I had the incredible privilege in February of sharing my story, along with 16 other women, at The Chapel Journeys Conference. The Director of Women's Ministries welcomed all who attended with these words: "These two days will be unlike any you've experienced in the church. Life is difficult, and every journey is unique to each woman. Every journey is different, yet we all face painful circumstances in life that can rock our world. Often times we hide our pain as we trod along the path by pretending or trying to look good. It's difficult to allow others to see the limp in our walk, so we pretend, put on a fake smile and say everything is OK. No more pretending! We're on the Journey of trust together. We're glad you've decided to join us. We invite you to relax, set aside any pre-conceived notions. Don't think about the woman beside you or compare yourself to anyone. This is your personal journey—alone, but together. You'll find God has always been right beside you along the way."

The weekend was awesome, and the experience of sharing my struggles and victories, my sorrows and joys with women was so amazing! I want to thank, with all of my heart, each one of you who prayed for me. I could not have done this without your prayers. God did a miraculous work in my life. *There was no spirit of fear whatsoever!* Yes, I was nervous, and my mouth felt like it had cotton in it. My hands shook. But God removed *all fear,* replacing it with *freedom and power.* So astonishing! It was equally astonishing to me that women actually wanted to hear my story, that they were interested in my journey. Me, the shy girl who escaped into books, making believe she was anyone other than who she really was. I don't say that with a sense of pride. It is such a humbling concept. Only Jesus could do that, for He is the Author and Hero of my story. It is my prayer that each woman who sat in on my sessions heard that clearly. And that as they listened to my journey of faith, they recognized the thread of love and redemption, mercy and grace the Savior has woven throughout my story thus far.

April 2008

Irish blood runs through my veins. I am enchanted by all things Irish—even the word itself sends a thrill through my heart.

Have you ever had a hope realized? Seen a dream come true? My dad's dream of some day visiting Ireland never happened because death stole it away on a June day in 1968. I picked up his torch and carried it with me for 33 years until on a June day in 2001 our dream was fulfilled. My daughter Hester was finishing up a semester of study in England. My husband Steve, our son Micah, and I were on a short furlough in the U.S. during our fourth term of missionary service in the Philippines. Months before our trip home to Ohio I had started day-dreaming about the possibility of flying to England and then taking a ferry to Ireland with Hester. Before I knew it, much to my amazement, my day-dream became a reality. I flew into London from Cleveland (through Toronto) and rode a bus to Cheltenham. Then two days later we took a train to Wales, where we caught a ferry. I remember so vividly the stirring in my soul when I captured my first glimpse of the Emerald Isle. As the land of my ancestors became visible out of the mist, bittersweet tears trickled down my cheek, while hauntingly beautiful Irish music played in the background on the ferry. A delicious chill then ran up and down my spine as I stepped onto Irish soil at Dun Laoghaire. I was in Ireland! From there we traveled by bus to Dublin, the city where my Grandfather McDermott was born in 1875. Standing at the rail along the River Liffey the next day, I just kept thinking with astonishment, *Am I really walking the very same streets that my grandfather walked as a child?* I tried to visualize what he looked like. I never knew him—he died when my dad was only two or three years old. A small picture of him as a young man living in Pennsylvania hangs on my family room wall. He's the handsome one in the front row, on the far right!

But I wanted to imagine him as a boy, running through the streets of Dublin. When Hester and I took a day trip to Howth Harbor the following day, I wondered if he had ever visited the seaside town. Did he walk up the hills lined with charming cottages? Did he run through the fields lush with heather? Did he sit on the cliffs looking out over the Irish Sea, pensively reflecting on his life? Did he stroll along the shore, picking up sea glass, curious where it came from? All these questions go unanswered.

The trip was much too short. I'd go back in a heartbeat. For now I soak up my Irish heritage in any way I can. *Through music:* The strains of Celtic music flowing from an Irish flute create a melancholy beauty that almost always sparks an emotional response from me. The mournful music and lyrics of "Danny Boy" are heart-rending. Of course, there are lively tunes that make me want to stand up and do an Irish jig! But I resist the urge. *Through movies:* One of my favorite Sunday afternoon pastimes is sitting in front of my television watching old Bing Crosby movies—"Going My Way" (1944) and "The Bells of St. Mary's" (1945), in which he portrayed Father O'Malley, an Irish Catholic priest. Barry Fitzgerald is in the first movie. I absolutely love his Irish brogue. He's so adorable when he chuckles and has that Irish twinkle in his eyes that I just want to give him a big hug. *Through books:* If I can get my hands on books about Ireland and the Irish, I'm a happy woman. B.J. Hoff wrote a series of novels called An Emerald Ballad. She quickly became my favorite Christian author.

Last fall I was introduced to *The Path of Celtic Prayer* by Calvin Miller. The author spoke at a retreat that our pastors and wives attended. He is quite the Renaissance man! During one of the breaks, Steve and I were sitting on the porch of the resort. Mr. Miller and his wife were out for a walk and stopped to join us in the rocking chairs. He saw me reading his book and offered to sign it for me. During our conversation, we found out that he had spent time teaching in the Philippines and had visited many places that we were familiar with. There were even some acquaintances that we had in common. But back to the book. I was intrigued by the topic of Celtic prayer and in particular by what I read in the introduction of the book. Calvin Miller wrote about a personal experience - an "epiphany moment" as he crossed over to the Isle of Iona on a ferry. He spoke of the medieval people who had lived on the island thousands of years ago. These people, as they talked "with God in the wild wind and sea, had formed a view of God that sent missionaries around the known world." Mr. Miller was eager to find the passion, to discover again the flame that burned within them.

I was excited by the thought of "the mystical soul of Ireland" bringing me to "new insight into genuine spirituality"—helping me to draw into a deeper and more intimate relationship with my Creator. I am now reading, morning and evening, Mr. Miller's newest book, *Celtic Devotions*.

Just a few short days ago, the sound of traditional Irish music captivated me at the E.J. Thomas Hall. I went with friends to the performance of Riverdance—a spectacular Irish dance show. Everything about the production was sensational. The dancing was incredible. The singing was beautiful. The music was amazing—the Celtic charm of the Irish fiddle and the Bodhran (Irish drum) went straight to my heart. I watched with anticipation as a journey unfolded on the stage—starting with the ancient Celts…gradually moving on to the potato famine…leading to immigration and the exodus…arriving in the new land and life on the streets of New York…and eventually coming full circle with a return to Ireland. The narrator concluded in a passionate voice: "The immigrant's child stood on the old land, back home again." With tears in my eyes, I wanted to shout out: "Not the immigrant's child, but his granddaughter, because seven years ago I was the one who stood on the old land. Ireland, my grandfather's home!" It was such a personal, almost spiritual, moment for me. The evening was one that I will not forget. My Irish eyes (even though they are brown) are still sparkling with laughter.

May 2008

It's a surreal experience to be with someone as they enter eternity. Only four times in my life have I accompanied a person "up to the gate of death."

My husband, on the other hand, faces death issues on a regular basis. He's had to deal in the middle of the night with the suicide of a son. He's been called to the hospital after a horrific car accident. He's been asked to come to hospice after or during the decision to stop life support. He's prayed with someone who has just been diagnosed with a terminal illness. He's brought a sense of peace and calm in the midst of fear or uncertainty. He's spoken words of comfort and truth at many funerals. He's ministered to parents who have lost a precious child.

I am overwhelmed thinking about the things that Steve sees. As well, I marvel at his composure and ability to minister with grace and love. He can only do this as he walks closely with his Lord. God has truly gifted and enabled him to extend comfort when needed. A friend once said that Steve "reeks with compassion." I have had the opportunity to observe this man for many years. He is one of the most genuinely caring and compassionate people I know.

But this constant exposure to dying and grief can leave him sapped of energy and almost always affected emotionally. Steve has told me that every now and then, when he's had a particularly difficult day, he'll stop at the newborn nursery at the hospital to look at the babies. It's healing to be reminded of new life. There are days when he comes home exhausted. Sometimes he wants to talk. When he's quiet, I know it's been a really hard day. He'll lie down on the couch, turn on the television, and vegetate for awhile.

However, there are rewards in the midst of the pain. Introducing a man to Jesus. Holding the hand of a woman who, assured of salvation, is excited and ready to meet her Savior. Seeing answers to prayers. Building relationships.

Several months ago, the Lord brought a young couple into Steve's life. They were in a crisis following the birth of their daughter. This sweet little girl was born with many physical problems. But what a fighter she was. She held on as long as she could. Her life was short—only eight weeks in this world. In that brief amount of time, she touched the lives of many. News of her death reached Steve on a Sunday morning while he was teaching a class. He sat down and cried. He grieved even though he knew that she was safe with Jesus.

I attended the calling hours at the funeral home. Seeing that tiny body in a casket that was not much bigger than a suitcase was heart-wrenching for me. With tears in my eyes, I hugged the grieving parents, even though I had never met them before. Because they were part of Steve's world, they were part of mine. The mother clung to me and said, "Thank you for sharing your husband with us. We don't know what we would have done without him." I heard these same words from the father and from the grandparents.

A few months after the baby's death, we took the couple out for dinner. They told me how they and the nurses knew when Steve was in the hospital headed for the ICU. The baby's vital signs always improved when he was near. A second or two later, Steve would walk through the door. The baby seemed to know that he was coming to visit her. She always responded to his presence and to his voice when he prayed for her. It was like she had a special connection to him.

We may not always understand the whys of pain and death and grief. And we certainly don't look forward to experiencing the intense emotions that are associated with them. But we are called to trust the One who holds all life in His hands. As He faithfully walks with us through the valley of the shadow of death, He gives grace and strength and comfort. He then asks us to extend that same grace and strength and comfort to the people He brings into our lives. I received an e-mail several days ago from a friend whose husband died 17 months ago. It has not been easy. She grieves deeply and misses the man who was the love of her life. I'm sure my friend never envisioned or desired this path that the Lord has put her on. But she knows that He has a purpose for her life, and she is allowing Him to use her to bring care and comfort and hope to another woman who has recently found herself a widow.

Death is part of the journey of life. In most situations, a dreaded part. We consider it an enemy. But Christ, through His resurrection, has conquered the grave and opened the way for us to live eternally with Him. So ultimately, we know that victory over death has already been secured. It's the part of the journey that ushers us into the presence of the Lord—a most holy moment.

The telephone rang while I was sitting in front of my computer writing this letter. It was my friend calling. With tears of sorrow and joy she said, "Mary, Mom's gone. She's with Jesus." She had the privilege of being by her mother's side, accompanying her up to the gate of death, where she closed her eyes here on this earth and opened them in glory. It was a holy moment for both of them!

June 2008

What was a gorgeous spring day in Columbus, Ohio, would have been a chilly day in the Philippines. When the temperatures "plunged" into the 70s in that Southeast Asian country, it was time for us to get out the blankets. Everyone walking the streets of Manila wore a jacket or sweater.

We weren't walking the streets of Manila on Sunday, May 25, even though it seemed like we could have been. The familiar sounds of Tagalog reached our ears, intermingled with a myriad of other Asian languages. The aroma of pancit, lumpia, and other Asian delicacies wafted through the air. Crowds of dark-haired people swarmed around us. We were instantly transported back to the Philippines while we walked through a park in Ohio! Steve and I drove two-and-a-half hours south to Columbus for the Asian Festival. We met our daughter Hester and son-in-law Dale, watched a few dance shows together, and then went our separate ways to explore market booths, eat Filipino food, look at displays, watch sports, and listen to choirs.

It didn't feel at all strange to be in that environment. In fact, it felt kind of—good! I'll be the first to admit that I have been quite surprised by my feelings since we returned to the States in 2003. It was never a secret that while we lived in the Philippines, my heart seemed to always be yearning for home. But now that we are finally home, I sometimes feel a bit "home-sick" for the Philippines. I'm not sure I can fully explain it. I guess we couldn't live in a country for as long as we did without it influencing our lives and coloring how we view the world. As we established relationships and friendships with Filipinos over the years, we found a connection—a connection that remains to this day. Certain aspects of the culture impacted us and have undoubtedly contributed to the kind of people we are today.

If this is true of us as adults, how much more must children be affected by living in a culture other than their own. I see the effects in all four of our adult children in varying degrees. Some of it has to do with the amount of immersion they had into Philippine culture. Each reacted differently, depending on their ages and personalities. Regardless of their responses, there's no getting around the fact that they were affected by their years in the Philippines. Their time living in an Asian country, along with the unique experiences each one had, definitely played a part in their immersion back into their own culture.

"Go Girls," a missionary arm of the women's ministry at our church, recently had a shower for our missionaries. I had the opportunity to share with those present about the blessings we received from our ABF when we came home for furlough in 1990 after a stressful first term. My three daughters then shared their thoughts. (Before I write anything else, I just have to say that I was extremely proud of each one of them!) They told of how blessed they were by the love and care of family and friends. But they also talked about how that year at home was a painful and difficult year for them. They didn't gloss it over—they were honest about their feelings. In retrospect, they now see how God worked through that time, and they have marveled at His grace.

It's not easy being an MK (missionary kid), trying to go between two or more different cultures and find your place in the world. My friend Felicia, who, along with her husband and four children, served on the mission field in the Philippines with us, recently sent me an e-mail with the link to an article written by an MK who is now an adult. I got tears in my eyes reading of what this young man has gone through, what many MKs go through when they return to their "homeland." They truthfully do not know where home is supposed to be. They feel guilty if they consider their host country home rather than their birth country. What should be familiar when they leave the mission field isn't, because everything seems strange or has changed while they were gone. There's no frame of reference. They find it hard to connect or relate.

My friend Sally, another fellow missionary in the Philippines, told me that probably about a third of MKs wrestle with identity issues. She said that when she "attended the first adult MK conference in Chicago in 2000, the pain of unresolved identity was palpable. It was a great time of healing for many but emotionally intense." She also mentioned that she thought both of her sons would agree it took at least ten years for them to find comfort and "at homeness" in their American identity.

Observing where my daughters and my son are today, I believe they are doing well. But it hasn't been without pain or sacrifice. Their journeys have included anger, confusion, frustration, rejection, fear, and loneliness. It was difficult over the years as a mother to watch them go through hard times that were directly linked to their father's and my being missionaries. I remember an incident that took place when we had been in the Philippines only a few short weeks. Our 20-month-old son was attacked by a monkey and bitten seven times on the head. I was angry and yelled out to God, "We came here to serve You. And this is what You do? It's one thing to sacrifice me or my husband. But my children? They never even had a choice in all this."

There were other episodes that tore at my mother's heart. Knowing that our daughter cried herself to sleep at night in the dorm. Watching them say goodbye to friends that they might never see again. Having to leave my girls as they started college in the U.S. It was heart-wrenching for me to say goodbye and return to the Philippines without them. It seemed my heart was always torn in two.

But God, in His infinite wisdom, knew exactly the paths we each needed to walk. As I learned to trust Him through the years, and as I witnessed and experienced His grace at work, I became a firm believer that He does not waste any part of our lives, including our pain. And I am confident that He has not wasted the pain that my children as MKs have gone through. Steve and I have talked and prayed with them, and I think they have worked through their emotions, each in his or her own way. Our Redeemer has redeemed the bad memories and brought healing. And He has preserved the good memories—of wonderful family times, great friendships, incredible and exciting experiences.

Now that we are on the other side of that journey, we have all realized that our years in the Philippines contributed to our spiritual and emotional growth in remarkable ways. Living in another culture has enriched our lives and broadened our world views. God, who walked the journey with us, worked it all for good in our lives as we saw up close and personal how amazing He is.

Genesis 48:15

The God who has been my shepherd all my life to this day.

Deuteronomy 1:31

The LORD your God carried you, as a father carries his *daughter*, all the way you went until you reached this place.

Deuteronomy 31:8

The LORD Himself goes before you and will be with you; He will never leave you nor forsake you. Do not be afraid; do not be discouraged.

Deuteronomy 33:12

Let the beloved of the LORD rest secure in Him, for He shields *her* all day long, and the one the LORD loves rests between His shoulders.

2 Chronicles 16:9

The eyes of the LORD range throughout the earth to strengthen those whose hearts are fully committed to Him.

Psalm 4:8

I will lie down and sleep in peace, for You alone, O LORD, make me dwell in safety.

Psalm 18:16–19, 28

He reached down from on high and took hold of me; He drew me out of deep waters. He rescued me from my powerful enemy, from my foes, who were too strong for me. They confronted me in the day of my disaster, but the LORD was my support. He brought me out into a spacious place; He rescued me because He delighted in me. My God turns my darkness into light.

Psalm 27:1–3

The LORD is my light and my salvation—whom shall I fear? The LORD is the stronghold of my life—of whom shall I be afraid. Though evil men advance against me to devour my flesh, when my enemies and my foes attack me, they will stumble and fall. Though an army besiege me, my heart will not fear; though war break out against me, even then will I be confident.

Psalm 27:10 (NLT)

Even if my father and mother abandon me, The LORD will hold me close.

Psalm 32:1–2

Blessed is *she* whose transgressions are forgiven, whose sins are covered. Blessed is the *woman* whose sin the LORD does not count against *her*.

Psalm 34:4

I sought the LORD, and He answered me; He delivered me from all my fears.

Psalm 40:1–3

I waited patiently for the LORD; He turned to me and heard my cry. He lifted me out of the slimy pit, out of the mud and mire; He set my feet on a rock and gave me a firm place to stand. He put a new song in my mouth, a hymn of praise to our God.

Isaiah 1:18

Though your sins are like scarlet, they shall be as white as snow; though they are red as crimson, they shall be like wool.

Isaiah 26:3

You will keep in perfect peace *her* whose mind is steadfast, because *she* trusts in You.

Isaiah 38:17

Surely it was for my benefit that I suffered such anguish. In Your love You kept me from the pit of destruction; You have put all my sins behind Your back.

Isaiah 40:11

He tends His flock like a shepherd; He gathers the lambs in His arms and carries them close to His heart.

Isaiah 40:28–31

Do you not know? Have you not heard? The LORD is the everlasting God, the Creator of the ends of the earth. He will not grow tired or weary, and His understanding no one can fathom. He gives strength to the weary and increases the power of the weak. Even youths grow tired and weary, and young men stumble and fall; but those who hope in the LORD will renew their strength. They will soar on wings like eagles; they will run and not grow weary, they will walk and not be faint.

Isaiah 41:10

Do not fear, for I am with you; do not be dismayed, for I am your God. I will strengthen you and help you; I will uphold you with My righteous right hand.

Isaiah 43:18–19

Forget the former things; do not dwell on the past. See, I am doing a new thing!

Isaiah 45:3

I will give you the treasures of darkness, riches stored in secret places, so that you may know that I am the LORD.

Isaiah 46:4

Even to your old age and gray hairs I am He, I am He who will sustain you. I have made you and I will carry you; I will sustain you and I will rescue you.

Isaiah 49:16

See, I have engraved you on the palms of My hands.

Jeremiah 29:11

"I know the plans I have for you," declares the LORD, "plans to prosper you and not to harm you, plans to give you hope and a future."

Lamentations 3:22–23

Because of the LORD's great love we are not consumed, for His compassions never fail. They are new every morning; great is His faithfulness.

Lamentations 3:55–57

I called on Your name, O LORD, from the depths of the pit. You heard my plea: "Do not close Your ears to my cry for relief." You came near when I called You, and You said, "Do not fear."

John 3:16

For God so loved the world that He gave His one and only Son, that whoever believes in Him shall not perish but have eternal life.

John 8:31–36

To the Jews who had believed Him, Jesus said, "If you hold to My teaching, you are really My disciples. Then you will know the truth, and the truth will set you free." They answered Him, "We are Abraham's descendants and have never been slaves of anyone. How can You say that we shall be set free?" Jesus replied, "I tell you the truth, everyone who sins is a slave to sin. Now a slave has no permanent place in the family, but a *daughter* belongs to it forever. So if the Son sets you free, you will be free indeed.

Romans 5:1–5

Therefore, since we have been justified through faith, we have peace with God through our Lord Jesus Christ, through whom we have gained access by faith into this grace in which we now stand. And we rejoice in the hope of the glory of God. Not only so, but we also rejoice in our sufferings, because we know that suffering produces perseverance; perseverance, character, and character, hope. And hope does not disappoint us, because God has poured out His love into our hearts by the Holy Spirit, whom He has given us.

Romans 8:37–39

In all these things we are more than conquerors through Him who loved us. For I am convinced that neither death nor life, neither angels nor demons, neither the present nor the future, nor any powers, neither height nor depth, nor anything else in all creation, will be able to separate us from the love of God that is in Christ Jesus our Lord.

2 Corinthians 10:3–5

For though we live in the world, we do not wage war as the world does. The weapons we fight with are not the weapons of the world. On the contrary, they have divine power to demolish strongholds. We demolish arguments and every pretension that sets itself up against the knowledge of God, and we take captive every thought to make it obedient to Christ.

2 Corinthians 12:9–10

He said to me, "My grace is sufficient for you for My power is made perfect in weakness." Therefore I will boast all the more gladly about my weaknesses, so that Christ's power may rest on me. That is why, for Christ's sake, I delight in weaknesses, in insults, in hardships, in persecutions, in difficulties. For when I am weak, then I am strong.

Galatians 5:1

It is for freedom that Christ has set us free. Stand firm, then, and do not let yourselves be burdened again by a yoke of slavery.

Galatians 5:16

Live by the Spirit, and you will not gratify the desires of the sinful nature.

Ephesians 3:12

In Him and through faith in Him we may approach God with freedom and confidence.

Ephesians 3:16–19

I pray that out of His glorious riches He may strengthen you with power through His Spirit in your inner being, so that Christ may dwell in your hearts through faith. And I pray that you, being rooted and established in love, may have power, together with all the saints, to grasp how wide and long and high and deep is the love of Christ, and to know this love that surpasses knowledge—that you may be filled to the measure of all the fullness of God.

Ephesians 5:8

You were once darkness, but now you are light in the Lord.

Ephesians 6:10–18

Finally, be strong in the Lord and in His mighty power. Put on the full armor of God so that you can take your stand against the devil's schemes. For our struggle is not against flesh and blood, but against the rulers, against the authorities, against the powers of this dark world and against the spiritual forces of evil in the heavenly realms. Therefore put on the full armor of God, so that when the day of evil comes, you may be able to stand your ground, and after you have done everything, to stand. Stand firm then, with the belt of truth buckled around your waist, with the breastplate of righteousness in place, and with your feet fitted with the readiness that comes from the gospel of peace. In addition to all this, take up the shield of faith, with which you can extinguish all the flaming arrows of the evil one. Take the helmet of salvation and the sword of the Spirit, which is the word of God. And pray in the Spirit on all occasions with all kinds of prayers and requests. With this in mind, be alert and always keep on praying for all the saints.

Philippians 3:12–14

Not that I have already obtained all this, or have already been made perfect, but I press on to take hold of that for which Christ Jesus took hold of me. *Sisters,* I do not consider myself yet to have taken hold of it. But one thing I do: Forgetting what is behind and straining toward what is ahead, I press on toward the goal to win the prize for which God has called me heavenward in Christ Jesus.

Philippians 4:7

And the peace of God, which transcends all understanding, will guard your hearts and your minds in Christ Jesus.

Philippians 4:8–9

Finally, *sisters,* whatever is true, whatever is noble, whatever is right, whatever is pure, whatever is lovely, whatever is admirable—if anything is excellent or praiseworthy—think about such things. Whatever you have learned or received or heard from me, or seen in me—put into practice. And the God of peace will be with you.

Philippians 4:13

I can do everything through Him who gives me strength.

Colossians 2:13–15

When you were dead in your sins and in the uncircumcision of your sinful nature, God made you alive with Christ. He forgave us all our sins, having canceled the written code, with its regulations, that was against us and that stood opposed to us; He took it away, nailing it to the cross. And having disarmed the powers and authorities, He made a public spectacle of them, triumphing over them by the cross.

2 Thessalonians 3:3

The Lord is faithful, and He will strengthen and protect you from the evil one.

Hebrews 4:16

Let us then approach the throne of grace with confidence, so that we may receive mercy and find grace to help us in our time of need.

2 Peter 1:3

His divine power has given us everything we need for life and godliness through our knowledge of Him who called us by His own glory and goodness.

1 John 4:4

The one who is in you is greater than the one who is in the world.

1 John 4:18

There is no fear in love. But perfect love drives out fear.

(All italics of the female gender are mine.)

To order additional copies of this title call:
1-877-421-READ (7323)
or please visit our Web site at
www.pleasantwordbooks.com

If you enjoyed this quality custom-published book,
drop by our Web site for more books and information.

www.winepressgroup.com
"Your partner in custom publishing."

Printed in the United States
147100LV00002B/26/P

9 781414 112619